<u>*Rocket Reading International*</u>

American Rocket Math
Matemáticas de cohetes estadounidenses

Copyright/Derechos de autor:

Table of Contents

Book Overview

By working smarter in math, students will become mathematicians, architects, electricians, plumbers, surveyors who work on roads and bridges, construction workers, tellers at the bank, scientists, doctors, pilots, astronauts, law enforcement, and mechanics who work on cars.

Different areas of addiction are covered and a example in solving a problem is provided. Students may have an example of a new concept that is introduced on a workbook page. Addition, subtraction, multiplication, and division cover the different areas a student may struggle with in math.

All students must memorize the addition, subtraction, and multiplication facts. To succeed in math, a 100% is required on each mini test in addition. Next, each subtraction mini-test and multiplication mini-test require practice and memorization to score a 100%. All tests cover facts from one to nine facts. Mini tests cover 1-3, 4-5, 6-7 and 8-9. Most of the higher-level work pages follow the same format when it comes to working mini testing.

Answers to the workbook pages are in the back of American Rocket Math. Do not allow a student to look at the answers before working problems on a page. Never have a student work more than one page each day. It will cause a student who is struggling to not like math. Never have a student work math page if they have not mastered their facts at a 100%. They will not like math. Finger counting is time consuming.

Encouraging words help to build confidence. Encouraging words are brilliant, exceptional, admirable, superb, tremendous, premium are words to help generate confidence.

<u>Libro Descritpcion General</u>

Al trabajar de manera mas inteligente en matematicas, los estudiantes se convertiran en matematicos arquitectos electricistas, plomeros, topografos que trabajan en carreteras y puentes, trabajadores de la construccion, cajeros de bancos, cientificos, medicos, pilots, astronautas, agentes del orden y mecanicos que trabajan en carros.

Se cubren diferentes areas de suma y se proporciona una visualizacion u orienacion para resolver un problema. Los estudiantes pueden tener un ejemplo sobre un nuevo concepto que se introduce en una pagina del libro de trabajo. La suma, resta, la multiplicacion y la division cubren las diferentes areas con las que un estudiante puede tener dificultades en matematicas.

Todos los estudiantes deben memorizer las operaciones de suma, resta y multiplication. Para tener exito en matematicas, ademas se require un 100% en cada mini-prueba. A continuacion cada miniprueba de resta y miniprueba de multiplicacion requierem practica y memorizacion para obtener una punctuacion del 100%. Todas las pruebas cubren hechos del uno al nueve hechos. Las mini pruebas cubren 1-3, 4-5, 6-7 y 8-9. La mayoria de las paginas de trabajo de nivel superior siguen el mismo formato cuando se trata de minipagomas de trabajo.

Las respuestas a las paginas del libro de trabajo se encuentran en la parte posterior de American Rocket Math. No permit que un estudiante mire las respuestas antes de resolver los problemas en una pagina. Nunca haga que un estudiante trabaje mas de una pagina por dia. Hara que a un estydiante que tiene dificultades no le gusten las matematicas. Nunca haga quee un estudiante trabaje paginas de matematicas si no ha dominado su operacion at 100%.

Palabras alentadoras son brillante, excepcional, admirable, soberbio, tremendo, de primera son palabras para ayudar a generar.

<u>Parent Notes:</u>

What should an adult observe in a child concerning math?

That a child does not count on their fingers in addition, subtraction, or multiplication. There are several signs to observe when they try to hide finger counting.

Make index cards segmented to match what you are working on, don't make all cards at once.

- Students cleverly use both hands at their side to count with their fingers.
- Hands behind their back counting.
- One hand covering the hand that has counting using their fingertips.
- Hands under the table make counting by fingers unnoticeable.
- Tips of fingers barely moving may not be observed.

<u>Notas para los padres:</u>

¿Qué debe observar un adulto en un niño con respecto a las matemáticas?

Que un niño no cuente con los dedos en la suma, la resta, o la multiplicación. Hay varias señales que observar cuando intentan ocultar el conteo con los dedos.

Haz fichas segmentadas para que coincidan con lo que estás trabajando, no hagas todas las fichas a la vez.
- Los estudiantes usan habilmente ambas manos a los lados para contar con los dedos.
- Manos detras de su espalda contando.
- Una mano cubriendo la mano que está contando usando la punta de sus dedos.
- Las manos debajo de la mesa hacen que contar con los dedos sea imperceptile.
- Es posible que no se noten las puntas de los dedos que apenas se mueven.

American Rocket Math Addition Chart

0 + 0 0	0 + 1 1	0 + 2 2	0 + 3 3	0 + 4 4	0 + 5 5	0 + 6 6	0 + 7 7	0 + 8 8	0 + 9 9
1 + 0 1	1 + 1 2	1 + 2 3	1 + 3 4	1 + 4 5	1 + 5 6	1 + 6 7	1 + 7 8	1 + 8 9	1 + 9 10
2 + 0 2	2 + 1 3	2 + 2 4	2 + 3 5	2 + 4 6	2 + 5 7	2 + 6 8	2 + 7 9	2 + 8 10	2 + 9 11
3 + 0 3	3 + 1 4	3 + 2 5	3 + 3 6	3 + 4 7	3 + 5 8	3 + 6 9	3 + 7 10	3 + 8 11	3 + 9 12
4 + 0 4	4 + 1 5	4 + 2 6	4 + 3 7	4 + 4 8	4 + 5 9	4 + 6 10	4 + 7 11	4 + 8 12	4 + 9 13
5 + 0 5	5 + 1 6	5 + 2 7	5 + 3 8	5 + 4 9	5 + 5 10	5 + 6 11	5 + 7 12	5 + 8 13	5 + 9 14
6 + 0 6	6 + 1 7	6 + 2 8	6 + 3 9	6 + 4 10	6 + 5 11	6 + 6 12	6 + 7 13	6 + 8 14	6 + 9 15
7 + 0 7	7 + 1 8	7 + 2 9	7 + 3 10	7 + 4 11	7 + 5 12	7 + 6 13	7 + 7 14	7 + 8 15	7 + 9 16
8 + 0 8	8 + 1 9	8 + 2 10	8 + 3 11	8 + 4 12	8 + 5 13	8 + 6 14	8 + 7 15	8 + 8 16	8 + 9 17
9 + 0 9	9 + 1 10	9 + 2 11	9 + 3 12	9 + 4 13	9 + 5 14	9 + 6 15	9 + 7 16	9 + 8 17	9 + 9 18

American Rocket Math Subtraction Chart

0 - 0 0	1 - 1 0								
2 - 0 2	2 - 1 1	2 - 2 0							
3 - 0 3	3 - 1 2	3 - 2 1	3 - 3 0						
4 - 0 4	4 - 1 3	4 - 2 2	4 - 3 1	4 - 4 0					
5 - 0 5	5 - 1 4	5 - 2 3	5 - 3 2	5 - 4 1	5 - 5 0				
6 - 0 6	6 - 1 5	6 - 2 4	6 - 3 3	6 - 4 2	6 - 5 1	6 - 6 0			
7 - 0 7	7 - 1 6	7 - 2 5	7 - 3 4	7 - 4 3	7 - 5 2	7 - 6 1	7 - 7 0		
8 - 0 8	8 - 1 7	8 - 2 6	8 - 3 5	8 - 4 4	8 - 5 3	8 - 6 2	8 - 7 1	8 - 8 0	
9 - 0 9	9 - 1 8	9 - 2 7	9 - 3 6	9 - 4 5	9 - 5 4	9 - 6 3	9 - 7 2	9 - 8 1	9 - 9 0

American Rocket Math Multiplication Chart

0 x 0 0	0 x 1 0	0 x 2 0	0 x 3 0	0 x 4 0	0 x 5 0	0 x 6 0	0 x 7 0	0 x 8 0	0 x 9 0
2 x 0 0	2 x 1 2	2 x 2 4	2 x 3 6	2 x 4 8	2 x 5 10	2 x 6 12	2 x 7 14	2 x 8 16	2 x 9 18
3 x 0 0	3 x 1 3	3 x 2 6	3 x 3 9	3 x 4 12	3 x 5 15	3 x 6 18	3 x 7 21	3 x 8 24	3 x 9 27
4 x 0 0	4 x 1 4	4 x 2 8	4 x 3 12	4 x 4 16	4 x 5 20	4 x 6 24	4 x 7 28	4 x 8 32	4 x 9 36
5 x 0 0	5 x 1 5	5 x 2 10	5 x 3 15	5 x 4 20	5 x 5 25	5 x 6 30	5 x 7 35	5 x 8 40	5 x 9 45
6 x 0 0	6 x 1 6	6 x 2 12	6 x 3 18	6 x 4 24	6 x 5 30	6 x 6 36	6 x 7 42	6 x 8 48	6 x 9 54
7 x 0 0	7 x 1 7	7 x 2 14	7 x 3 21	7 x 4 28	7 x 5 35	7 x 6 42	7 x 7 49	7 x 8 56	7 x 9 63
8 x 0 0	8 x 1 8	8 x 2 16	8 x 3 24	8 x 4 32	8 x 5 40	8 x 6 48	8 x 7 56	8 x 8 64	8 x 9 72
9 x 0 0	9 x 1 9	9 x 2 18	9 x 3 27	9 x 4 36	9 x 5 45	9 x 6 54	9 x 7 63	9 x 8 72	9 x 9 81

1. uno	20. veinte	39. treinta y nueve
2. dos	21. veintiuno	40. cuarenta
3. tres	22. veintidós	41. cuarenta y uno
4. cuatro	23. veintitrés	42. cuarenta y dos
5. cinco	24. veinticuatro	43. cuarenta y tres
6. seis	25. veinticinco	44. cuarenta y cuatro
7. siete	26. veintiséis	45. cuarenta y cinco
8. ocho	27. veintisiete	46. cuarenta y seis
9. nueve	28. veintiocho	47. cuarenta y siete
10. diez	29. veintinueve	48. cuarenta y ocho
11. once	30. trentea	49. cuarenta y nueve
12. doce	31 treinta y uno	50. cincuenta
13. trece	32. treinta y dos	51. cincuenta y uno
14. catore	33. treinta y tres	52. cincuenta y dos
15. quince	34. treinta y cuatro	53. cincuenta y tres
16. dieciseis	35. treinta y cinco	54. cincuenta y cuatro
17. diecisiete	36. treinta y seis	55. cincuenta y cinco
18. dieciocho	37. treinta y sieta	56. cincuenta y seis
19. diecinueve	38. treinta y ocho	57. cincuenta y siete

58. cincuenta y ocho	77. setenta y siete	96. noventa y seis
59. cincueta y ocho	78. setenta y ocho	97. noventa y siete
60. sesenta	79. setenta y nueve	98. noventa y ocho
61. sesenta y uno	80. ochenta	99. noventa y nueve
62. sesenta y dos	81. ochenta y uno	100. cien
63. sesenta y tres	82. ochenta y dos	101. ciento uno
64. sesenta y cuatro	83. ochenta y tres	102. ciento dos
65. sesenta y cinco	84. ochenta y cuatro	103. ciento tres
66. sesenta y seis	85. ochenta y cinco	104. ciento cuatro
67. sesenta y siete	86. ochenta y seis	105. ciento cinco
68. sesenta y ocho	87. ochenta y siete	106. ciento seis
69.sesenta y nueve	88. ochenta y ocho	107. ciento siete
70. setenta	89. ochenta y nueve	108. ciento ocho
71. setenta y uno	90. noventa	109. ciento nueve
72. setenta y dos	91. noventa y uno	110. ciento diez
73. setenta y tres	92. noventa y dos	111. ciento once
74. setenta y cuatro	93. noventa y tres	112. ciento doce
75. setenta y cinco	94. noventa y cuatro	113. ciento trece
76. setenta y seis	95. noventa y cinco	114. ciento catorce

115. ciento quince	134. ciento treinta y cuatro	153. ciento cincuenta y tres
116. ciento dieciséis	135. Ciento treinta y cinco	154. ciento cincuenta y cuatro
117. ciento diecisiete	136. ciento treinta y seis	155. ciento cincuenta y cinco
118. ciento dieiocho	137. ciento treinta y siete	156. ciento cincuenta y seis
119. ciento diecinueve	138. ciento treinta y ocho	157. ciento cincuenta y siete
120. ciento veinte	139. ciento treinta y nueve	158. ciento cincuenta y ocho
121. ciento veintiuno	140. ciento cuarenta	159. ciento cincuenta y nueve
122. ciento veintidós	141. ciento cuarenta y uno	160. ciento sesenta
123. ciento veintitrés	142. ciento cuarenta y dos	161. ciento sesenta y uno
124. ciento veinticuatro	143. ciento cuarenta y tres	162. ciento sesenta y dos
125. ciento veinticinco	144. ciento cuarenta y cuatro	163. ciento sesenta y tres
126. ciento veintideis	145. ciento cuarenta y cinco	164. ciento sesenta y cuatro
127. ciento veintisiete	146. ciento cuarenta y seis	165. ciento sesenta y cinco
128. ciento veintiocho	147. ciento cuarenta y siete	166. ciento sesenta y seis
129. ciento veintinueve	148. ciento cuarenta y ocho	167. ciento sesenta y siete
130. ciento treinta	149. ciento cuarenta y nueve	168. ciento sesenta y ocho
131. ciento treinta y uno	150. ciento cincuenta	169. ciento sesenta y nueve
132. ciento treinta y dos	151. ciento cincuenta y uno	170. ciento setenta
133. ciento treinta y tres	152. ciento cincuenta y dos	171. ciento setenta y uno

Instructor Addition Page

1,2,3,4,5,6,7,8,9 are whole numbers. Two numbers added together are called addends. The answer to the addends are called the sum. On the front of one card write 1+0=?. On the front of another index card write 0+1=?. On the backside of the index card include the equation and the answer. Numbers can be written vertical or horizontal. An option is shown below.

Use a lot of positive comments while teaching or coaching your child. Great, wonderful, excellent, super, fabulous, marvelous. Superior, superb, splendid, remarkable, cool, spectacular, amazing, and impressive.

<table>
<tr><td>

Frontside

$1+0=?$ $0+1=?$

$$\begin{array}{r} 1 \\ +\ 0 \\ \hline ? \end{array} \qquad \begin{array}{r} 0 \\ +\ 1 \\ \hline ? \end{array}$$

</td><td>

Backside

$0+1=1$ $1+0=1$

$$\begin{array}{r} 0 \\ +\ 1 \\ \hline 1 \end{array} \qquad \begin{array}{r} 1 \\ +\ 0 \\ \hline 1 \end{array}$$

</td></tr>
</table>

Two rapid snaps of an adult's fingertips is enough time allotted for a student to answer the equation presented on an index card. A student must pass the oral addition test quickly before taking a paper test that is timed.

Addition paper test 1-3.

Addition paper test 4-5.

Addition paper test 6-7.

Addition paper test 8-9.

In teaching the nine addition facts, students will find there is a pattern to learning the nines. Nine is the larger number. The smaller number will be added to the nine but will be one less than the smaller number. There will always be two numbers, but the second number will be one less than the addition fact. Examples are shown below.

$9+1=10$	$9+2=11$	$9+3=12$	$9+4=13$	$9+5=14$
$9+6=15$	$9+7=16$	$9+8=17$	$9+9=18$	

*****

<u>*Página de adicion de instructores*</u>

1,2,3,4,5,6,7,8,9 son numeros enteros. Dos numeros sumados se llaman sumandos. La respuesta a los sumandos se llama suma. ¿En el frente de una tarjeta escribe 0+1=? En el frente de otra tarjeta incluye la suma vertical horizontal. Vea abajo.

Usa muchos comentarios positivos mientras enseñas a su nené. Esto ayudara desarrollar la confianza del estudiante mientras, aprende las operaciones matemáticas. Por ejemplo, genial, maravilloso, excelente, super, fabuloso, superior, soberbio, esplendido, notable, fría, espectacular, sorprendente, e impresionante.

Lado delantero		*Trasero*	
$1+0=?$ $0+1=?$		$1+0=1$ $0+1=1$	
$\begin{array}{r} 1 \\ +\,0 \\ \hline ? \end{array}$ $\begin{array}{r} 0 \\ +\,1 \\ \hline ? \end{array}$		$\begin{array}{r} 1 \\ +\,0 \\ \hline 1 \end{array}$ $\begin{array}{r} 0 \\ +\,1 \\ \hline 1 \end{array}$	

Dos chasquidos dedos de un adulto es tiempo suficiente para que un estudiante responda la ecuación presentada en una tarjeta. Un estudiante debe aprobar la prueba oral de suma rápidamente antes de tomar una prueba en papel cronometrada.

Prueba de papel adicional 1-3.
Prueba de papel adicional 4-5.
Prueba de papel adicional 6-7.
Prueba de papel adicional 8-9.

Al enseñar las nueve operaciones de suma los estudiantes encontraran que existe un patrón para aprender los nueve. Nueve es el número menor se sumará al nueve, pero será uno menos que la suma. A continuación, se muestran ejemplos.

9+1=10   9+2=11   9+3=12   9+4=13

9+5=14   9+6=15   9+7=16   9+8=17

9+9=18

American Rocket Math Test Addition 0-3
Prueba de Suma de American Rocket Math 0-3
1st grade 2 minutes – 2 minuto primer grado 100% accuracy
1 minute for older students – 1 minuto para estudiantes mayores- 100% accuracy.

1 + 0	1 + 3	3 + 4	3 + 7	2 + 6	1 + 5
3 + 2	2 + 4	3 + 0	2 + 7	3 + 6	2 + 2
6 + 1	2 + 8	5 + 2	3 + 8	2 + 9	1 + 8
3 + 3	1 + 4	3 + 5	3 + 9	1 + 1	8 + 3
0 + 2	1 + 7	1 + 9	3 + 7	1 + 2	9 + 3

American Rocket Math Test Addition 4-5
Prueba de Suma de American Rocket Math 4-5
1st grade 2 minutes – 2 minuto primer grado 100% accuracy
1 minute for older students – 1 minuto para estudiantes mayores- 100% accuracy.

$\begin{array}{r} 8 \\ +\ 4 \\ \hline \end{array}$	$\begin{array}{r} 5 \\ +\ 5 \\ \hline \end{array}$	$\begin{array}{r} 7 \\ +\ 4 \\ \hline \end{array}$	$\begin{array}{r} 8 \\ +\ 5 \\ \hline \end{array}$	$\begin{array}{r} 4 \\ +\ 4 \\ \hline \end{array}$
$\begin{array}{r} 6 \\ +\ 5 \\ \hline \end{array}$	$\begin{array}{r} 3 \\ +\ 4 \\ \hline \end{array}$	$\begin{array}{r} 7 \\ +\ 5 \\ \hline \end{array}$	$\begin{array}{r} 5 \\ +\ 4 \\ \hline \end{array}$	$\begin{array}{r} 3 \\ +\ 5 \\ \hline \end{array}$
$\begin{array}{r} 2 \\ +\ 4 \\ \hline \end{array}$	$\begin{array}{r} 6 \\ +\ 4 \\ \hline \end{array}$	$\begin{array}{r} 1 \\ +\ 5 \\ \hline \end{array}$	$\begin{array}{r} 2 \\ +\ 5 \\ \hline \end{array}$	$\begin{array}{r} 9 \\ +\ 4 \\ \hline \end{array}$
$\begin{array}{r} 4 \\ +\ 5 \\ \hline \end{array}$	$\begin{array}{r} 1 \\ +\ 4 \\ \hline \end{array}$	$\begin{array}{r} 0 \\ +\ 5 \\ \hline \end{array}$	$\begin{array}{r} 9 \\ +\ 5 \\ \hline \end{array}$	$\begin{array}{r} 0 \\ +\ 4 \\ \hline \end{array}$

American Rocket Math Test Addition 6-7
Prueba de Suma de American Rocket Math 6-7
1st grade 2 minutes – 2 minuto primer grado 100% accuracy
1 minute for older students – 1 minuto para estudiantes mayores- 100% accuracy.

7	4	3	9	5
+ 6	+ 7	+ 6	+ 7	+ 6

7	4	2	5	2
+ 7	+ 6	+ 6	+ 7	+ 7

0	8	9	6	0
+ 6	+ 7	+ 6	+ 6	+ 7

1	1	3	8	6
+ 7	+ 6	+ 7	+ 6	+ 7

American Rocket Math Test Addition 8-9
Prueba de Suma de American Rocket Math 8-9
1ˢᵗ grade 2 minutes – 2 minuto primer grado 100% accuracy
1 minute for older students – 1 minuto para estudiantes mayores- 100% accuracy.

0 + 8	9 + 9	5 + 8	4 + 9	7 + 8
7 + 9	2 + 9	8 + 8	3 + 9	4 + 8
1 + 9	6 + 9	0 + 9	1 + 8	9 + 8
5 + 9	6 + 8	8 + 9	3 + 8	2 + 8

Instructor Page Subtraction

There are fifty-four subtraction facts to learn. Every student will need to be challenged in their thinking skills when it comes to math. If taught the pattern for finding the answer, the student will feel confident working with math numbers. On one index card write the equation with no answer in front (9-2=?). Then on the opposite side of the index card, write the subtraction fact with the answer (9-2=7).

The larger numbers are on top is called the minuend. The smaller number is underneath the larger number called the subtrahend. The total is called the difference. The following steps teach how to prove the answer is correct.

The first example shows a subtraction problem with a missing digit. In step two we have a traditional problem. In step three and four, there are two ways to prove 2 is the correct answer. By adding 2+7=9 and 7+2=9. In the first example we subtract the difference from the minuend when a question mark is seen (?) as shown in step one and two below. The answer is 2.

1.		2.		3.	4.
9	minuend	9	min.	2	7
- ?	subtrahend	- 7	sub.	+ 7	+ 2
7	difference	2	dif.	9	9

Página de subastación de Instructor

Hay cincuenta y cuatro operaciones de resta que aprender. Cada estudiante deberá ser desafiado en sus habilidades de pensamiento cuando se trata de matemáticas. Si se le enseñas el patrón para encontrar la respuesta, el estudiante disfrutará de las matemáticas y se sentirá seguro trabajando con numeros matemáticos. En una tarjeta respuesta. Luego en el lado opuesto de la tarjeta, escribe la resta con la respuesta.

Los números más grandes que están en la parte superior se llaman minuedo. El número más pequeño está debajo del número más grande llamado sustraendo. El total se llama diferencia. Los siguientes pasos enseñan cómo demostrar que la respuesta es correcta.

El primer ejemplo muestra un problema de resta con un dígito faltante. En el segundo paso tenemos un problema tradicional. En los pasos tres y cuatro, hay dos formas de demostrar que 2 es la respuesta correcta. Sumando 2+7=9 y 7+2=9. En el primer ejemplo, restamos la diferencia del minuendo cuando se ve un signo de interrogación (?) como se muestra en los pasos uno y dos a continuación. La respuesta es 2.

1.   9 minuendo
   - ? sustraendo
   7 diferencia
	2. 9 min.
	   - 7 sum.
	   2 dif.
		3. 2 sumando
		   + 7 sumando
		   9 suma
			4. 7
			   + 2
			   9

American Rocket Math Test Subtraction 0-3
Prueba de matemáticas American Rocket Resta 0-3
1st grade 30 seconds – 100% accuracy 30 segundos primer grado 100% exactitude.
15 seconds for older students – 15 segundos para estudiantes mayores para.

3	3	2	3	2
- 3	- 1	- 2	- 0	- 0

2	3	1	1	0
- 1	- 2	- 0	- 1	- 0

American Rocket Math Test Subtraction 4-5
Prueba de matemáticas American Rocket Resta 4-5
1ˢᵗ grade 30 seconds – 100% accuracy 30 segundos primer grado 100% exactitude.
15 seconds for older students – 15 segundos para estudiantes mayores para.

$$\begin{array}{cccc}
5 & 4 & 5 & 4 \\
-\,2 & -\,2 & -\,4 & -\,0 \\
\hline
\end{array}$$

$$\begin{array}{cccc}
4 & 5 & 4 & 4 \\
-\,1 & -\,1 & -\,3 & -\,4 \\
\hline
\end{array}$$

$$\begin{array}{ccc}
5 & 5 & 5 \\
-\,0 & -\,3 & -\,5 \\
\hline
\end{array}$$

American Rocket Math Test Subtraction 6-7
Prueba de matemáticas American Rocket Resta 6-7
1st grade 30 seconds – 100% accuracy 30 segundos primer grado 100% exactitude.
15 seconds for older students – 15 segundos para estudiantes mayores para.

6 − 2	7 − 3	6 − 5	7 − 0	6 − 1
7 − 5	6 − 0	7 − 6	7 − 1	6 − 6
6 − 4	7 − 2	6 − 3	7 − 7	7 − 4

American Rocket Math Test Subtraction 8-9
Prueba de matemáticas American Rocket Resta 8-9
1st grade 30 seconds – 100% accuracy 30 segundos primer grado 100% exactitude.
15 seconds for older students – 15 segundos para estudiantes mayores para.

8 − 2	9 − 3	8 − 4	9 − 5	8 − 6
9 − 2	9 − 6	8 − 7	9 − 9	8 − 1
9 − 7	8 − 5	9 − 8	9 − 1	8 − 3
9 − 2	8 − 8	9 − 4	8 − 0	

Instructors Multiplication Page

Multiplication is a higher-level math for students. Third grade will study and learn the multiplication tables up to nine. Fourth grade will study ten through twelve multiplication facts. Therefore, the students profile folder must be passed to the fourth-grade teacher.

Our main or top number is called the multiplicand. The second or bottom number is called the multiplier. The total is the product. Multiplication gets confused with addition often, and there are some similarities, but large differences.

Skip counting can be useful in the beginning. Some students may even confuse multiplication with addition when a zero is involved. A zero in an addition fact will add up to a whole number (8+0 =8). A zero multiplied by a whole number will have a zero for the answer every time (8x0=0).

Analytical thinking occurs in math when multiplication facts trade spaces with the numbers. On the front of an index card, write the equation without the answer. On another index card write the same equation without the answer by trading spaces with the numbers.

Frontside	
1. 7 x 6 ?	2. 6 x 7 ?

Backside	
1. 7 multiplicand x 6 multiplier 42 product	2. 6 x 7 42

What is the secret about learning the fives multiplication tables? In multiplication, the fives will always end in 0 or 5. And all even numbers will end in 0.

Example: **2x5=1̲0, 4**x5= 2̲0, 5x5=25, 7x5=35

In the answer, the first number of the product will be half the amount of the even number. Even numbers are 2,4,6,8,0. Examples like **2̲**x5=**1̲**0 or 4x5=20. Odd numbers are **3,5,7,9** and will end in a 5 if being multiplied. Example: 3x5=1**5̲** 5x5=2**5̲.**

However, in the nine's multiplication tables, the answer will be one less than the even and odd numbers. Examples below:

9x2=**1̲**8   9x3=**2̲**7   9x4=**3̲**6   9x5=**4̲**5

9x7=**6̲**3   9x8=**7̲**2   9x9=**8̲**1   9x**6̲**=**5̲**4

Just as previously notes write the equation on one side of an index card and answer on the back. Examples are shown.

<table>
<tr><td>Frontside</td><td></td><td>Backside</td><td></td></tr>
<tr><td colspan="4">horizontal</td></tr>
<tr><td>1. 9x2=?</td><td>2. 2x9=?</td><td>1. 9x2=18</td><td>2. 2x9=18</td></tr>
</table>

<u>Página de Multiplicación de Instructores</u>

La multiplicación es una matemática de nivel superior para los estudiantes. El tercer grado estudiará y aprenderá las tablas de multiplicar hasta el nueve. El cuarto grado estudiará las multiplicaciones de diez a doce. Por lo tanto, la carpeta de perfil de los estudiantes debe pasarse al maestro de cuarto grado.

Nuestro número principal o superior se llama multiplicando. El segundo número o número inferior se llama multiplicador. El total es el producto. La multiplicación se confunde a menudo con la suma, y hay algunas similitudes, pero grandes diferencias.

Saltar el conteo puede ser útil al principio. Algunos estudiantes pueden incluso confundir la multiplicación con la suma cuando se trata de un cero. Un cero en una suma sumará un número entero (8+0 =8). Un cero multiplicado por un número entero tendrá un cero para la respuesta cada vez (8x0=0).

El pensamiento analítico ocurre en matemáticas cuando las operaciones de multiplicación intercambian espacios con los números. En el anverso de una ficha, escribe la ecuación sin la respuesta. En otra ficha, escribe la misma ecuación sin la respuesta intercambiando espacios con los números.

Lado delantero		**Trasero**	

1.   7
   <u>x 6</u>
   ?
	2. 6
	   <u>x 7</u>
	   ?
		1. 7 multiplicando
		   <u>x 6</u> multiplicador
		   42 producto
			2. 6
			   <u>x 7</u>
			   42

¿Cuál es el secreto de aprender las tablas de multiplicar de cincos? En la multiplicación, los cincos siempre terminarán en 0 o 5. Y todos los números pares terminarán en 0.

Ejemplo: **2**x5=<u>1</u>0, **4**x5= <u>2</u>0, 5x5=2**5**, 7x5=3**5**

En la respuesta, el primer número del producto será la mitad de la cantidad del número par. Los números pares son **2,4,6,8,0**. Ejemplos como 2x5=10 o 4x5=20. Los números impares son **3,5,7,9** y terminarán en un 5 si se multiplican.

Ejemplo: **3**x5=15 **5**x5=25

Sin embargo, en las tablas de multiplicar del nueve, la respuesta será uno menos que los números pares e impares. Ejemplos a continuación:

9x2=<u>1</u>8	9x3=<u>2</u>7	9x4=<u>3</u>6	9x5=<u>4</u>5
9x6=<u>5</u>4	9x7=<u>6</u>3	9x8=<u>7</u>2	9x9=<u>8</u>1

Al igual que las notas anteriores, escriba la ecuación en un lado de una tarjeta y responda en el reverso. Se muestran ejemplos.

<table>
<tr><td colspan="2">Lado delantero</td><td colspan="2">Trasero</td></tr>
<tr><td colspan="4" align="center">Horizontal</td></tr>
<tr><td>1. 9x2=?</td><td>2. 2x9=?</td><td>1. 9x2=18</td><td>2. 2x9=18</td></tr>
</table>

American Rocket Multiplication Test 0-3
Multiplicación de cohetes americanos 0-3
1 minute 100% accuracy—1 minuto 100% precision

2 x 1	3 x 3	2 x 5	1 x 7	0 x 5	8 x 3
2 x 3	3 x 8	2 x 2	3 x 4	2 x 4	3 x 6
3 x 3	2 x 6	6 x 3	3 x 7	0 x 3	1 x 3
2 x 7	2 x 9	2 x 8	5 x 3	2 x 0	3 x 2
3 x 5	0 x 4	3 x 4	3 x 1	3 x 9	3 x 7

American Rocket Multiplication Test 4-5
Multiplicacio de cohetes Americanos 4-5
1 minute 100% accuracy—1 minuto 100% precision

1	3	0	5	7	5
x 5	x 4	x 4	x 5	x 5	x 4

5	3	7	6	4	4
x 8	x 5	x 4	x 5	x 6	x 8

5	4	8	1	0	8
x 6	x 4	x 4	x 4	x 5	x 5

4	2	5	4	9	4
x 6	x 4	x 2	x 5	x 5	x 9

American Rocket Multiplication Test 6-7
Multiplicación de cohetes Americanos 6-7
1 minute 100% accuracy—1 minuto 100% precision

6 x 1	7 x 3	6 x 4	0 x 6	5 x 6
7 x 5	6 x 6	4 x 7	7 x 7	8 x 7
9 x 7	7 x 1	6 x 9	6 x 8	7 x 6
6 x 2	7 x 7	0 x 7	2 x 7	6 x 3

American Rocket Multiplication Test 8-9
Multiplicación de cohetes Americanos 8-9
1 minute 100% accuracy—1 minuto 100% precision

0 x 8	9 x 2	8 x 8	9 x 6	9 x 3
7 x 9	8 x 6	4 x 8	8 x 7	5 x 9
0 x 9	8 x 1	8 x 5	9 x 9	8 x 9
8 x 2	9 x 1	3 x 8	4 x 9	9 x 9

Tens-Twelve Table
Mesa Diez-Doce

10	10	10	10	10	10	10	10	10	10	10	10	10
x 0	x 1	x 2	x 3	x 4	x 5	x 6	x 7	x 8	x 9	x10	x11	x12
0	10	20	30	40	50	60	70	80	90	100	110	120

11	11	11	11	11	11	11	11	11	11	11	11	11
x 0	x 1	x 2	x 3	x 4	x 5	x 6	x 7	x 8	x 9	x10	x11	x12
0	11	22	33	44	55	66	77	88	99	110	121	132

12	12	12	12	12	12	12	12	12	12	12	12	12
x 0	x 1	x 2	x 3	x 4	x 5	x 6	x 7	x 8	x 9	x10	x11	x12
0	12	24	36	48	60	72	84	96	108	120	132	144

American Rocket Multiplication Test 10-12
Multiplicación de cohetes Americanos 10-12
1 minute 100% accuracy—1 minuto 100% precision

12 x 0	11 x 4	10 x 5	11 x 6	12 x 4	12 x 6	12 x 3
12 x 11	11 x 1	11 x 5	10 x 10	10 x 2	10 x 7	11 x 2
12 x 4	12 x 7	12 x 1	11 x 0	10 x 9	11 x 3	11 x 7
10 x 11	12 x 2	10 x 6	11 x 12	11 x 10	10 x 4	11 x 9
11 x 8	10 x 12	10 x 3	12 x 10	11 x 11	12 x 9	12 x 12
12 x 5	10 x 8	10 x 0	10 x 1	12 x 8		

American Rocket Multiplication Test 3-12
Multiplicacio de cohetes Americanos 3-12
1 minute 100% accuracy—1 minuto 100% precision

3	4	8	9	11	12	10
x 3	x 7	x 5	x 8	x 11	x 4	x 6

7	6	10	7	11	9	6
x 6	x 8	x 11	x 7	x 12	x 4	x 7

12	6	7	9	8	4	7
x 10	x 9	x 3	x 7	x 8	x 6	x 9

8	3	8	3	4	10	12
x 7	x 6	x 4	x 8	x 9	x 7	x 8

9	6	5	4	7	12	10
x 9	x 6	x 9	x 4	x 5	x 12	x 12

5	9	4	5	4	12	11
x 5	x 3	x 3	x 6	x 5	x 6	x 9

<u>Simple Word Problems-Mixed</u>
Problemas de palabras simples-Mixto
~On The Farm~
Have students show how they solved the problem. Use paper or white board.

1. Rob had 26 chickens. He bought 45 more chickens. How many chickens does Rob have now?

2. Frank had 47 pigs. He sold 25 pigs. How many pigs does Frank have now?

3. Mallard ducks cost $2.00 each. How much will 5 ducks cost Jill when she buys them?

4. Joe has 15 cats to keep mice away from his wheat farm. He bought 14 more cats. How many cats does Joe have now?

5. Dave has 3 dogs. Strangers dropped off 7 dogs on his road. How many dogs does Dave have if he adopts them?

-Spanish Version-
~En la granja~
** Pida a los estudiantes que muestren cómo resolvieron el problema. Utilice papel o pizarra blanca.**

1. Rob tenía 26 pollos. Compró 45 pollos más. ¿Cuántas gallinas tiene Rob ahora?

2. Frank tenía 47 cerdos. Vendió 25 cerdos. ¿Cuántos cerdos tiene Frank ahora?

3. Los patos reales cuestan $ 2.00 cada uno. ¿Cuánto le costarán 5 patos a Jill cuando los compre?

4. Joe tiene 15 gatos para mantener a los ratones alejados de su granja de trigo. Compró 14 gatos más. ¿Cuántos gatos tiene Joe ahora?

5. Dave tiene 3 perros. Unos desconocidos dejaron 7 perros en su camino. ¿Cuántos perros tiene Dave si los adopta?

~Trees~
Have students show how they solved the problem. Use paper or white board.

1. Bill has 28 walnut trees. He bought 48 walnut trees. How many trees does Bill have now?

2. James will harvest 36 almond trees this fall. He added 48 new almond trees. How many trees will James's harvest?

3. Franks farm planted 19 pistachio trees. Frank wants to buy 28 more pistachio trees. How many trees will he have in all?

4. John hired 38 men to help harvest trees. He needs 45 men in all to harvest his crop. How many men does John still need?

5. Grass grows under the trees. 10 men and women were hired to clear the weeds. A total of 28 people is needed. How many people are still needed?

-Spanish Version-
~Árboles~
Pida a los estudiantes que muestren cómo resolvieron el problema. Utilice papel o pizarra blanca.

1. Bill tiene 28 nogales. Compró 48 nogales. ¿Cuántos árboles tiene Bill ahora?

2. James cosechará 36 almendros este otoño. Añadió 48 nuevos almendros. ¿Cuántos árboles cosechará James?

3. La granja Franks plantó 19 árboles de pistacho. ¿Frank quiere comprar 28 pistachos más. ¿Cuántos árboles tendrá en total?

4. Juan contrató a 38 hombres para ayudar a cosechar árboles. Necesita 45 hombres en total para cosechar su cosecha. ¿Cuántos hombres necesita Juan todavía?

5. La hierba crece debajo de los árboles. Se contrataron 10 hombres y mujeres para limpiar la maleza. Se necesitan un total de 28 personas. ¿Cuántas personas aún se necesitan?

~Super Store~

Have students show how they solved the problem. Use paper or white board.

1. Bob has 48 packages of bubble gum. He gave 28 packages of gum away on Monday. How much does Bob have left?

2. Joe has 98 basketballs. He sold 48 basketballs on Tuesday. How many basketballs did not sell?

3. Harry has 19 car kits. He needs 28 car kits. How many car kits will he need to buy?

4. Jason bought 59 toy soldiers. He needs 75 soldiers in all. How many toys does Jason still need?

5. Charlie wanted 29 candy bars for his school project. He had 3 bars at home. How many more candy bars are needed?

-Spanish Version-
~Súper Tienda~

*** Pida a los estudiantes que muestren cómo resolvieron el problema. Utilice papel o pizarra blanca. ***

1. Bob tiene 48 paquetes de chicle. El lunes regaló 28 paquetes de chicles. ¿Cuánto le queda a Bob?

2. Joe tiene 98 balones de baloncesto. Vendió 48 balones de baloncesto el martes. ¿Cuántas pelotas de baloncesto no se vendieron?

3. Harry tiene 19 kits de autos. Necesita 28 kits de coches. ¿Cuántos kits de coche tendrá que comprar?

4. Jason compró 59 soldaditos de juguete. Necesita 75 soldados en total. ¿Cuántos juguetes necesita Jason?

5. Charlie quería 29 barras de chocolate para su proyecto escolar. Tenía 3 bares en casa. ¿Cuántas barras de chocolate más se necesitan?

~Farmers Market~
Have students show how they solved the problem. Use paper or white board.

1. Ted had 39 baskets of strawberries. Three baskets had bad strawberries. He had to throw the 3 baskets away. How many baskets of strawberries does Ted have left?

2. Lucy hired two clerks to help sell the produce. One of the clerks sold 35 watermelons. The second clerk sold 46 watermelons. How many watermelons were sold altogether.

3. 2 cantaloupes were sold on Monday. 3 cantaloupes were sold on Tuesday. 8 cantaloupes were sold on Wednesday. How many cantaloupes were sold in three days?

4. June sold 4 groups of onions. 5 long stemmed onions are in each group. What was the total number of onions that sold?

5. 15 tomatoes sold on Saturday. 82 tomatoes sold on Sunday. How many tomatoes sold that weekend?

-Spanish Version-
~Mercado de agricultores~
** Pida a los estudiantes que muestren cómo resolvieron el problema. Utilice papel o pizarra blanca.**

1. Ted tenía 39 canastas de fresas. Tres canastas tenían fresas en mal estado. Tuvo que tirar las 3 canastas. ¿Cuántas cestas de fresas le quedan a Ted?

2. Lucy contrató a dos empleados para que le ayudaran a vender los productos. Uno de los empleados vendió 35 sandías. El segundo empleado vendió 46 sandías. Cuántas sandías se vendieron en total.

3. El lunes se vendieron 2 melones. El martes se vendieron 3 melones. El miércoles se vendieron 8 melones. ¿Cuántos melones se vendieron en tres días?

4. Junio vendió 4 grupos de cebollas. Hay 5 cebollas de tallo largo en cada grupo. ¿Cuál fue el número total de cebollas que se vendieron?

5. 15 tomates vendidos el sábado. 82 tomates vendidos el domingo. ¿Cuántos tomates se vendieron ese fin de semana?

~Grocery Store~
Have students show how they solved the problem. Use paper or white board.

1. A pound of apples cost $2.59. How much would 7 pounds of apples cost?

2. Sugar costs $8.45 for a big sack. What will it cost for 9 sacks?

3. Tide detergent costs $19.99 for a large box. How much will it cost to purchase 7 boxes of Tide?

4. A box of eggs will cost $4.95. How much will it cost to buy 8 cartons of eggs.

5. A box of cake mix costs $3.39. How much will 3 boxes of cake mix cost?

-Spanish Version-
~Abacería~
Pida a los estudiantes que muestren cómo resolvieron el problema. Utilice papel o pizarra blanca.

1. Una libra de manzanas cuesta $2.59. ¿Cuánto costarían 7 libras de manzanas?

2. El azúcar cuesta $8.45 por un saco grande. ¿Cuánto costarán 9 sacos?

3. El detergente Tide cuesta $19.99 por una caja grande. ¿Cuánto costará comprar 7 cajas de Tide?

4. Una caja de huevos costará $4.95. ¿Cuánto costará comprar 8 cartones de huevos?

5. Una caja de mezcla para pastel cuesta $3.39. ¿Cuánto costarán 3 cajas de mezcla para pastel?

~The Big Garden~
Have students show how they solved the problem. Use paper or white board.

1. Tim wants to plant pumpkins seeds. He has 9 bags of pumpkin seeds. Tim needs twice the number of seeds. How many bags will Tim have to plant once he gets them?

2. Tom has 15 bags of cantaloupe seeds. He is short 5 bag of seeds. How many bags will Tom have to plant cantaloupe?

3. If the cost of planting watermelon seeds is $1,500.00 per acre. How much will it cost for 5 acres to be planted?

4. An acre of tomato seeds is $1,840.00 per acre. How much will it cost to plant 6 acres of tomato seeds.

5. Dan decided to plant one onion. From one seed, 3 onion bulbs will grow. How many onions will Dan get when he plants 5 onion seeds?

-Spanish Version-
~El Gran Jardín~
Pida a los estudiantes que muestren cómo resolvieron el problema. Utilice papel o pizarra blanca.

1. Tim quiere plantar semillas de calabaza para hacer crecer su jardín. Tiene 9 bolsas de semillas de calabaza. Tim necesita el doble de semillas. ¿Cuántas bolsas tendrá que plantar Tim una vez que las tenga?

2. Tom tiene 15 bolsas de semillas de melón. Le faltan 5 bolsas de semillas. ¿Cuántas bolsas tendrá Tom para plantar melón?

3. Si el costo de plantar semillas de sandía es de $1,500.00 por acre. ¿Cuánto costará plantar 5 acres?

4. Un acre de semillas de tomate cuesta $1840.00 por acre. ¿Cuánto costará plantar 6 acres de semillas de tomate?

5. Dan decidió plantar una cebolla. De una semilla, crecerán 3 bulbos de cebolla. ¿Cuántas cebollas obtendrá Dan cuando plante 5 semillas de cebolla?

~Chips and More Chips~
Have students show how they solved the problem. Use paper or white board.

1. Sam wants to plant 3 rows of corn. He has 15 plants to plant. How many will be planted in each row?

2. Jerry wants to disk his land to plant clover. It will take him 10 hours to disk his field. Jerry has spent 2 hours disking so far. How many hours will it take Jerry to finish disking?

3. If Nick has 30 corn chip packages and he wants each friend to get an equal amount of chips. He has 6 friends. How many bags will each friend get?

4. There are 48 bags of potato chips. How many bags of potato chips will 6 children take home?

5. Fred has 30 students on his field trip. He wants 5 rows of students. How many students will he place in each row?

-Spanish Version-
~Fichas y más fichas~
*** Pida a los estudiantes que muestren cómo resolvieron el problema. Utilice papel o pizarra blanca.***

1. Sam quiere plantar 3 hileras de maíz. Tiene 15 plantas para plantar. ¿Cuántos se plantarán en cada hilera?

2. Jerry quiere dedicar su tierra a plantar tréboles. Le llevará 10 horas grabar su campo. Jerry ha pasado 2 horas haciendo discking hasta ahora. ¿Cuántas horas tardará Jerry en terminar de desalojar?

3. Si Nick tiene 30 paquetes de papas fritas de maíz y quiere que cada amigo reciba la misma cantidad de papas fritas. Tiene 6 amigos. ¿Cuántas bolsas recibirá cada amigo?

4. Hay 48 bolsas de papas fritas. ¿Cuántas bolsas de papas fritas se llevarán a casa 6 niños?

5. Fred tiene 30 estudiantes en su excursión. Quiere 5 filas de estudiantes. ¿Cuántos estudiantes colocará en cada fila?

<ins>Instructions in Addition and Missing Numbers</ins>

Before beginning to add harder concepts into addition, subtraction, multiplication or division, students must show mastery at 100% in each area of math facts. Students will being to like math when mastery of facts prove to be hundred percent. Therefore, once a first grader can work the simple single and double-digit numbers with 100% mastery, they may be introduced to find the missing number concepts. As an adult, you will find practice pages at different grade levels. Students in third grade and fourth grade have material to work.

Small numbers do not have 2 digits in the answer. A larger number added to a smaller number will have a two digit-sum. When adding small numbers, the sum has a single digit. However, the larger number that is added to another higher number will have a two-digit sum. After adding the tens column both digits are written down.

Reading the numbers begin from left to right, but working with numbers to solve a problem begins with the far-right number.

There are some pages on finding the missing number. First in A add all the numbers above the finish line to find a sum. Next, place the sum number from A under the finish line on top beside B. Then place the sum you found in the addition from A and place it underneath the original sum that was below the finish line. Subtract to find the answer. Write the missing fact number near the letter C. If correct, your new number will be placed into A and the addition will be correct.

1.	5 4 M + 6 ――― 25	**A.** 5 4 + 6 ――― 15	**B.** 25 - 15 ――― 10	**C.** 10

First, a student will have two-digits plus one digit. Some will not have any carrying involved. Other problems with larger numbers will have carrying involved. Two-digit addition facts plus two-digit addition facts are introduced. Students will quickly realize carrying is involved with solving the problems. Next, students advance to adding two-digits but have three rows of two-facts to solve.

There will be 3 rows of two-digit problems to solve and carrying is required. Addition is taken a step further by having students solve three rows of 3-digit numbers.

Instrucciones sobre la suma y los números que faltan

Antes de comenzar a agregar conceptos más difíciles a la suma, resta, multiplicación o división, los estudiantes deben demostrar un dominio del 100% en cada área de las operaciones matemáticas. A los estudiantes les gustarán las matemáticas cuando el dominio de los hechos demuestre ser cien por cien. Por lo tanto, una vez que un niño de primer grado puede trabajar los números simples de uno y dos dígitos con un dominio del 100%, se le puede presentar para encontrar los conceptos de números que faltan. Como adulto, encontrará páginas de práctica en diferentes niveles de grado. Los estudiantes de tercer y cuarto grado tienen material para trabajar.

Por lo tanto, un niño de primer grado será capaz de trabajar los números simples de uno y dos dígitos. Pueden ser introducidos para encontrar el número que falta. Como adulto, encontrará páginas de práctica en diferentes niveles de grado. Los estudiantes de tercer y cuarto grado tienen material para trabajar.

Los números pequeños no tienen 2 dígitos en la respuesta. Un número más grande sumado a un número más pequeño tendrá una suma de dos dígitos. Al sumar números pequeños, la suma tiene un solo dígito. Sin embargo, el número más grande que se sume a otro número más alto tendrá una suma de dos dígitos. Después de sumar la columna de decenas, se escriben ambos dígitos.

La lectura de los números comienza de izquierda a derecha, pero el trabajo con números para resolver un problema comienza con el número de la extrema derecha.

Hay algunas páginas sobre cómo encontrar el número que falta. Primero en A suma todos los números por encima de la línea de meta para encontrar una suma. A continuación, coloque el número de suma de A debajo de la línea de meta en la parte superior al lado de B. Luego coloca la suma que encontraste en la suma de A y colócala debajo de la suma original que estaba debajo de la línea de meta. Resta para encontrar la respuesta. Escribe el número de dato que falta cerca de la letra C. Si es correcto, su nuevo número se colocará en A y la adición será correcta.

1.	5	A.	5	B.	25	C.	10
	4		4		- 15		
	M		+ 6		10		
	+ 6		15				
	25						

Primero, un estudiante tendrá dos dígitos más un dígito. Algunos no tendrán ningún acarreo involucrado. Otros problemas con números más grandes tendrán que ver con el acarreo. Se introducen las operaciones de suma de dos dígitos más las de suma de dos dígitos. Los estudiantes se darán cuenta rápidamente de que llevar está involucrado en la resolución de los problemas. A continuación, los estudiantes avanzan para sumar dos dígitos, pero tienen tres filas de dos hechos para resolver.

Habrá 3 filas de problemas de dos dígitos para resolver y se requiere transporte. La suma se lleva un paso más allá al hacer que los estudiantes resuelvan tres filas de números de 3 dígitos.

~2 Digits Plus One Digit-#1-3~
~2 digitos mas 1 digitos~

1. 10
  + 1

2. 11
  + 1

3. 12
  + 1

4. 11
  + 2

5. 22
  + 3

6. 10
  + 2

7. 13
  + 1

8. 11
  + 3

9. 11
  + 1

10. 12
  + 3

11. 13
  + 3

12. 10
  + 3

13. 23
  + 3

14. 30
  + 1

15. 21
  + 3

16. 31
  + 3

17. 33
  + 3

18. 32
  + 3

19. 20
  + 2

20. 30
  + 3

~2 Digits Plus One Digit …4-5~
2 digitos mas 1 digitos

1. 23 + 4	**2.** 15 + 1	**3.** 30 + 4	**4.** 54 + 5	**5.** 43 + 4
6. 53 + 5	**7.** 41 + 4	**8.** 45 + 4	**9.** 42 + 4	**10.** 14 + 4
11. 24 + 5	**12.** 51 + 5	**13.** 31 + 4	**14.** 21 + 5	**15.** 22 + 5
16. 22 + 4	**17.** 32 + 4	**18.** 25 + 4	**19.** 44 + 5	**20.** 55 + 4

~2 Digit Plus One Digit ...6-7~
2 digitos mas 1 digitos

1. 45 + 6	**2.** 37 + 5	**3.** 26 + 5	**4.** 47 + 6	**5.** 73 + 7
6. 26 + 7	**7.** 56 + 7	**8.** 74 + 7	**9.** 55 + 7	**10.** 74 + 6
11. 65 + 6	**12.** 57 + 7	**13.** 64 + 6	**14.** 75 + 7	**15.** 53 + 7
16. 76 + 6	**17.** 58 + 7	**18.** 79 + 7	**19.** 46 + 6	**20.** 75 + 7

1. 99 + 9	**2.** 54 + 8	**3.** 75 + 9	**4.** 86 + 8	**5.** 58 + 9
6. 89 + 8	**7.** 67 + 9	**8.** 68 + 8	**9.** 74 + 8	**10.** 92 + 9
11. 96 + 9	**12.** 75 + 8	**13.** 93 + 8	**14.** 72 + 8	**15.** 43 + 9
16. 84 + 9	**7.** 91 + 9	**18.** 32 + 8	**19.** 87 + 8	**20.** 57 + 8

~*Addition- 2 Digits Plus 2 Digits #1*~
2 digitos mas 2 digitos

1. 54 + 98	**2.** 73 + 29	**3.** 87 + 24	**4.** 64 + 16
5. 68 + 47	**6.** 22 + 49	**7.** 82 + 99	**8.** 53 + 89
9. 23 + 48	**10.** 85 + 57	**11.** 63 + 48	**12.** 96 + 25

~*Addition-2 Digits Plus 2 Digit #2*~

2 digitos mas 2 digitos

1. 95
+ 47

2. 43
+ 28

3. 54
+ 36

4. 63
+ 47

5. 67
+ 19

6. 84
+ 27

7. 75
+ 67

8. 84
+ 26

9. 46
+ 25

10. 83
+ 27

11. 46
+ 37

12. 58
+ 29

2 digitos mas 2 digitos

1. 45
\+ 29

2. 72
\+ 28

3. 65
\+ 49

4. 73
\+ 29

5. 56
\+ 27

6. 86
\+ 39

7. 57
\+ 64

8. 82
\+ 29

9. 73
\+ 29

10. 68
\+ 27

11. 93
\+ 49

12. 86
\+ 79

~3 Rows of 2 Digit Addition #1~
3 filas de suma de 2 digitos

1. 43
  25
+ 78
	2. 64
	  71
	+ 29
		3. 52
		  88
		+ 35
			4. 75
			  32
			+ 68

5. 47
  81
+ 35
	6. 62
	  55
	+ 35
		7. 39
		  47
		+ 62
			8. 48
			  29
			+ 15

9. 23
  78
+ 41
	10. 56
	  29
	+ 48
		11. 46
		  28
		+ 19
			12. 86
			  75
			+ 34

~3 Rows of 2 Digit Addition #2~
3 filas de suma de 2 digitos

1. 36 42 + 59	**2.** 75 46 + 28	**3.** 52 34 + 53	**4.** 44 36 + 91
5. 61 25 + 38	**6.** 73 42 + 16	**7.** 45 23 + 45	**8.** 63 45 + 86
9. 36 21 + 53	**10.** 52 43 + 87	**11.** 64 33 + 86	**12.** 65 49 + 97

~3 Rows of 2 Digit Addition #3~
3 filas de suma de 2 digits

1. 43
     27
+ 61
	2. 83
	     24
	+ 78
		3. 62
		     37
		+ 84
			4. 43
			     29
			+ 48

5. 47
     64
+ 61
	6. 32
	     41
	+ 75
		7. 86
		     41
		+ 23
			8. 65
			     29
			+ 34

9. 75
     39
+ 41
	10. 83
	      24
	+ 98
		11. 64
		      29
		+ 87
			12. 57
			      48
			+ 93

~*Ones and Tens Carrying in Addition #1*~

Unos y decenas llevan ademas

1. 125
+ 476

2. 354
+ 869

3. 593
+ 127

4. 527
+ 193

5. 417
+ 196

6. 643
+ 279

7. 293
+ 148

8. 346
+ 197

9. 976
+ 326

10. 458
+ 375

~Ones and Tens Carrying in Addition #2~

Unos y decenas llevan ademas

1. 643
\+ 157

2. 798
\+ 222

3. 648
\+ 179

4. 526
\+ 395

5. 478
\+ 196

6. 356
\+ 377

7. 492
\+ 318

8. 483
\+ 197

9. 546
\+ 199

10. 743
\+ 297

~Ones and Tens Carrying in Addition #3~
Unos y decenas llevan ademas

1. 342 + 179	**2.** 794 + 297	**3.** 743 + 295	**4.** 648 + 297
5. 748 + 297	**6.** 846 + 379	**7.** 244 + 197	**8.** 846 + 288
9. 347 + 299	**10.** 643 + 279		

~Ones and Tens Carrying in Addition Advanced #1~
Unos y decenas llevan ademas avanzada

1. 135	**2.** 347	**3.** 649	**4.** 596
769	639	467	286
+ 213	+ 543	+ 298	+ 345

5. 742	**6.** 456	**7.** 265	**8.** 547
989	452	432	293
+ 654	+ 598	+ 679	+ 417

9. 864	**10.** 658
376	492
+ 298	+ 765

~*Ones and Tens Carry in Addition Advanced #2*~
Unos y decenas llevan ademas avanzada

1. 345
   264
+ 342

2. 723
   417
+ 863

3. 543
   378
+ 417

4. 795
   264
+ 384

5. 437
   298
+ 541

6. 724
   634
+ 282

7. 246
   359
+ 847

8. 523
   149
+ 286

9. 543
   123
+ 478

10. 898
   645
+ 783

~Ones and Tens Carry in Addition Advanced #3~
Unos y decenas llevan ademas avanzada

1. 643 256 + 841	**2.** 786 243 + 144	**3.** 659 832 + 142	**4.** 645 298 + 346
5. 754 293 + 846	**6.** 298 346 + 849	**7.** 298 341 + 782	**8.** 346 429 + 823
9. 842 129 + 648	**10.** 756 291 + 456		

~*Prove the Answer 2 Ways #1*~
~ Pruebe la respuesta de 2 maneras # 1 ~

Directions: Solve the problem and prove 2 ways the answer is correct.

Instrucciones: Resuelva el problema y demuestre 2 formas en que la respuesta es correcta

	Example:	A.	B.
	3 + 5 ――― 8	8 - 5 ――― 3	8 - 3 ――― 5

1. 4
+ 2   **A.**   **B.**

2. 8
+ 5   **A.**   **B.**

3. 2
+ 9   **A.**   **B.**

4. 8
+ 5   **A.**   **B.**

~*Prove the Answer 2 Ways #2*~
~ Pruebe la respuesta de 2 maneras # 2 ~

Directions: Solve the problem and prove 2 ways the answer is correct.

Instrucciones: Resuelva el problema y demuestre 2 formas en que la respuesta es correcta

1. 4
   + 8   **A.**   **B.**

2. 6
   + 7   **A.**   **B.**

3. 4
   + 9   **A.**   **B.**

4. 5
   + 8   **A.**   **B.**

5. 8
   + 9   **A.**   **B.**

~ Pruebe la respuesta de 2 maneras # 3 ~

Directions: Solve the problem and prove 2 ways the answer is correct.

Instrucciones: Resuelva el problema y demuestre 2 formas en que la respuesta es correcta

1. 1
  + 7

         A.   **B.**

2. 4
  + 5

         A.   **B.**

3. 6
  + 8

         A.   **B.**

4. 7
  + 8

         A.   **B.**

5. 9
  + 8

         A.   **B.**

~*Addition/Subtraction: Find the Missing Number #1*~

~Suma/Resta: Encuentra el número que falta #1~

Directions: Find the missing number. Prove answer and write answer near the letter B. ~*Instrucciones: Encuentra el número que falta. Pruebe la respuesta y escriba la respuesta cerca de la letra B.

Example:	$\begin{array}{r} 8 \\ +\ M \\ \hline 17 \end{array}$	**A.** $\begin{array}{r} 17 \\ -\ 8 \\ \hline 9 \end{array}$	**B.** 9

1. $\begin{array}{r} 38 \\ +\ M \\ \hline 47 \end{array}$ **A.**   **B.**

2. $\begin{array}{r} 85 \\ +\ M \\ \hline 101 \end{array}$ **A.**   **B.**

3. $\begin{array}{r} 76 \\ +\ M \\ \hline 93 \end{array}$ **A.**   **B.**

4. $\begin{array}{r} 45 \\ +\ M \\ \hline 101 \end{array}$ **A.**   **B.**

5. $\begin{array}{r} 79 \\ +\ M \\ \hline 145 \end{array}$ **A.**   **B.**

~*Addition/Subtraction: Find the Missing Number #2*~

~*Suma/Resta: Encuentra el número que falta #2*~

Directions: Find the missing number. Prove answer and write answer near the letter B. ~*Instrucciones: Encuentra el número que falta. Pruebe la respuesta y escriba la respuesta cerca de la letra B.

1. 36
  + M
   73
          A.   **B.**

2. 43
  + M
   78
          A.   **B.**

3. 28
  + M
   97
          A.   **B.**

4. 83
  + M
   99
          A.   **B.**

5. 23
  + M
   47
          A.   **B.**

~*Addition/Subtraction: Find the Missing Number #3*~
~Suma/Resta: Encuentra el número que falta #3~

*Directions: Find the missing number. Prove answer and write answer near the letter B. ~*Instrucciones: Encuentra el número que falta. Pruebe la respuesta y escriba la respuesta cerca de la letra B.*

1. 73
 + M
   89

A.   B.

2. 64
 + M
  101

A.   B.

3. 17
 + M
   38

A.   B.

4. 23
 + M
   46

A.   B.

5. 84
 + M
   99

A.   B.

Advanced Find the Missing Number #1
Avanzada Encuentra el número que falta #1

***Add all numbers in A. Subtract A total from original sum in B. Solve for M in C*/**
Suma todos los números en A. Resta el total de A de la suma original en B. Resuelve M en C

Example:
```
   5
   3
   M
+  9
  27
```
A. 5+3+9=17

B.
```
  27
-  17
  10
```
C. M=10

1.
```
   4
   5
   M
+  4
  26
```
A.

B.

C.

2.
```
   5
   9
   8
+  M
  31
```
A.

B.

C.

3.
```
   4
   M
   6
+  9
  43
```
A.

B.

C.

4.
```
   8
   9
   8
+  M
  58
```
A.

B.

C.

5.
```
   4
   M
   6
+  9
  78
```
A.

B.

C.

~*Advanced Find the Missing Number #2* ~
Avanzada Encuentra el número que falta #2

***Add all numbers in A. Subtract A total from original sum in B. Solve for M in C*/**
Suma todos los números en A. Resta el total de A de la suma original en B. Resuelve M en C

1. 8
    M
    3
    9
+ 7
  76

A.   **B.**   **C.**

2. 4
    5
    M
    6
+ 9
  80

A.   **B.**   **C.**

3. 9
    7
    3
+ M
  24

A.   **B.**   **C.**

4. 6
    4
    9
+ M
  33

A.   **B.**   **C.**

5. 7
    9
    6
    8
+ M
  44

A.   **B.**   **C.**

Add all numbers in A. Subtract A total from original sum in B. Solve for M in C/
Suma todos los números en A. Resta el total de A de la suma original en B. Resuelve M en C

1. 8   **A.**   **B.**   **C.**
    M
    3
+   9
‾‾‾‾
  76

2. 4   **A.**   **B.**   **C.**
    5
    M
    6
+   9
‾‾‾‾
  82

3. 9   **A.**   **B.**   **C.**
    7
    3
+   M
‾‾‾‾
  82

4. 6   **A.**   **B.**   **C.**
    4
    9
+   M
‾‾‾‾
  30

5. 7   **A.**   **B.**   **C.**
    9
    M
    6
+   8
‾‾‾‾
  45

Subtraction Overview

Subtraction begins with a single digit being subtracted from a 2-digit number that is the top number. A student will borrow from a whole number that is in the ten's column.

The next few pages introduce 2 digits being subtracted from 3 digits. Borrowing begins in the ten and next the hundredth column.

<table>
<tr><td>Example:</td><td></td><td></td><td></td></tr>
<tr><td></td><td></td><td>* 3</td><td>13</td><td></td></tr>
<tr><td></td><td>* 3312</td><td>* 3</td><td>3</td><td>12</td></tr>
<tr><td></td><td>442</td><td>4</td><td>4</td><td>2</td></tr>
<tr><td></td><td>- 45</td><td>-</td><td>4</td><td>5</td></tr>
<tr><td></td><td>397</td><td>3</td><td>9</td><td>7</td></tr>
</table>

These are the new numbers after you borrow from the tens and hundreds.

Next, a zero in the middle changes the zero into a 9 because a ten was stolen from the hundred's column. The ten is added to the single digit number on top. Adding the ten and the number makes it a tens number in the one's column.

<table>
<tr><td>Example:</td><td></td><td></td><td></td></tr>
<tr><td></td><td></td><td>4</td><td>9</td><td>17</td></tr>
<tr><td></td><td>507</td><td>5</td><td>0</td><td>7</td></tr>
<tr><td></td><td>- 9</td><td></td><td></td><td>9</td></tr>
<tr><td></td><td>498</td><td>4</td><td>9</td><td>8</td></tr>
</table>

It will not matter what number is underneath a zero. The pattern is the same. You will always borrow from a whole number. A teen in subtraction is considered to be from 10-19. There are three lessons.

There are many zeros involved in the next three examples.

Examples:

	A.	29910	B.	499910	C.	5999910
		3,000		50,000		600,000
		- 1		- 1		- 1
		2,999		49,999		599,999

Subtraction Worksheets Overview

- Single digit subtracts by 2 digits—by borrowing.

- Borrowing from 10's and 100's

- Borrowing from whole number with zero provided.

****

Descripción general de la resta

  La resta comienza con la resta de un solo dígito de un número de 2 dígitos que es el número superior. Un estudiante tomará prestado de un número entero que se encuentra en la columna de las decenas.

  En las páginas siguientes se presentan 2 dígitos que se restan de 3 dígitos. El préstamo comienza en la columna de diez y luego en la de centenas

Ejemplo:

		* 3	13	
* 3312		* 3	3	12
442		4	4	2
- 45		-	4	5
397		3	9	7

****Estos son los nuevos números después de tomar prestado de las decenas y las***

centenas.

A continuación, un cero en el medio cambia el cero por un 9 porque se robó un diez de la columna de la centena. El diez se suma al número de un solo dígito en la parte superior. Al sumar el diez y el número, se convierte en un número adolescente en la columna de unidades. No importará qué número esté debajo de un cero. El patrón es el mismo. Siempre tomarás prestado de un número entero. Se considera que un adolescente en sustracción tiene entre 10 y 19 años. Hay tres lecciones.

Hay muchos ceros involucrados en los siguientes tres ejemplos.

Ejemplo:

A.	29910	**B.**	499910	**C.**	5999910
	3,000		50,000		600,000
	− 1		− 1		− 1
	2,999		49,999		599,999

Descripción general de las hojas de trabajo de resta

- Un dígito resta por 2 dígitos, por préstamo
- Tomar prestado de 10 y 100
- Préstamo de números enteros con cero

~*Subtraction: Ones Borrow From Tens Column #1*~
~*Resta: Los Unos Toman Prestado de las Decenas Columna #1*~

1. 42 − 3	**2.** 53 − 4	**3.** 36 − 9	**4.** 75 − 6
5. 45 − 7	**6.** 81 − 2	**7.** 52 − 7	**8.** 73 − 4
9. 70 − 1	**10.** 44 − 6		

~*Subtraction: Ones Borrow From Tens Column #2*~
~*Resta: Los Unos Toman Prestado de las Decenas Columna #2*~

1. 34
  - 5

2. 26
  - 7

3. 84
  - 7

4. 93
  - 6

5. 85
  - 7

6. 63
  - 4

7. 52
  - 4

8. 33
  - 5

9. 61
  - 7

10. 80
  - 4

1. 91
− 2

2. 23
− 8

3. 54
− 6

4. 71
− 2

5. 74
− 7

6. 53
− 4

7. 75
− 6

8. 27
− 9

9. 38
− 9

10. 73
− 7

~*Subtraction: Borrowing From Tens & Hundreds Column #1*~

**Resta: prestamo de decenas y centenas. Tomando prestado de la columna de decenas y centenas*

1. 121
  - 75

2. 814
  - 27

3. 736
  - 47

4. 428
  - 79

5. 725
  - 46

6. 312
  - 36

7. 831
  - 54

8. 345
  - 26

9. 562
  - 63

10. 723
  - 84

~*Subtraction: Borrowing from Hundreds Column #1*~

Resta: Préstamo de Centenas Columna #1

Pattern will be the same even if the numbers change./
El patrón será el mismo incluso si los números cambian.

<table>
<tr><td>

Example/Ejemplos:

$$\begin{array}{r} 59[13] \\ 603 \\ -4 \\ \hline 599 \end{array} \qquad \begin{array}{r} 599 \\ +4 \\ \hline 603 \end{array}$$

Check answer by adding/Verifique la respuesta agregando

</td></tr>
</table>

***You must borrow from the largest number to successfully subtract. You take 1, or 10, from the 6. It becomes a 5, and you give that 1 to 0 making it 10. We take 1 from 10, making it a 9, and give that 1 ten to the 3. Making it 13. Now you can subtract 4 from 13.**

*** Debes pedir prestado del número más grande para restar con éxito. Tomas 1, o 10, del 6. Se convierte en un 5, y le das 1 a 0 convirtiéndolo en 10. Tomamos 1 de 10, convirtiéndolo en un 9, y le damos ese 1 diez al 3. Haciéndolo 13. Ahora puedes restar 4 de 13.**

1. 402 − 2	**2.** 803 − 4	**3.** 601 − 2	**4.** 504 − 5
5. 300 − 1	**6.** 401 − 3	**7.** 605 − 6	**8.** 306 − 7
9. 603 − 4	**10.** 707 − 9		

~<u>*Subtraction: Borrowing from Hundreds Column #2*</u>~

Resta: Préstamo de Centenas Columna #2

Pattern will be the same even if the numbers change./
El patrón será el mismo incluso si los números cambian.

1. 301 - 2	**2.** 407 - 8	**3.** 800 - 1	**4.** 800 - 2
5. 700 - 3	**6.** 403 - 8	**7.** 400 - 1	**8.** 604 - 7
9. 507 - 9	**10.** 604 - 7		

~Subtraction: Borrowing from Hundreds Column #3~

Resta: Préstamo de Centenas Columna #3

*Pattern will be the same even if the numbers change./
*El patrón será el mismo incluso si los números cambian.

1. 302
  -   5

2. 804
  -   5

3. 703
  -   4

4. 902
  -   3

5. 403
  -   8

6. 600
  -   1

7. 704
  -   6

8. 404
  -   5

9. 801
  -   3

10. 206
  -   7

~*Subtraction: Borrowing from Thousands Column #1*~
~*Resta: Pedir prestado de miles Columna #1*~

Pattern will be the same even if the numbers change. Additional numbers with zero will follow the same pattern as seen on an earlier page./
El patrón será el mismo incluso si los números cambian. Los números adicionales con cero seguirán el mismo patrón que se vio en una página anterior.

Example/Ejemplo:

$$
\begin{array}{r}
899[10] \\
9000 \\
-\quad 1 \\
\hline
8999
\end{array}
$$

---

1. 8,000
  - 1

2. 2,000
  - 2

3. 4,000
  - 1

4. 6,000
  - 3

5. 7,000
  - 4

6. 8,000
  - 6

7. 2,000
  - 8

8. 3,000
  - 7

9. 1,000
  - 5

10. 5,000
  - 9

~Subtraction: Borrowing from Ten Thousands Column #2~

~Resta: Préstamo de miles diez Columna #2~

Pattern will be the same even if the numbers change./
El patrón será el mismo incluso si los números cambian.

1. 60,000
   - 2

2. 80,000
   - 1

3. 50,000
   - 5

4. 90,000
   - 3

5. 30,000
   - 4

6. 10,000
   - 6

7. 70,000
   - 7

8. 40,000
   - 9

9. 20,000
   - 2

10. 60,000
    - 3

~Subtraction: Borrowing from Hundreds Column #3~
~Resta: Préstamo de Centenas Columna #3~
*Pattern will be the same even if the numbers change./
*El patrón será el mismo incluso si los números cambian.

1. 100,000
-           1

2. 700,000
-           2

3. 300,000
-           4

4. 400,000
-           5

5. 800,000
-           9

6. 200,000
-           3

7. 900,000
-           4

8. 600,000
-           7

9. 700,000
-           1

10. 500,000
-           5

~Subtraction:Tens Column Borrowing from Hundreds #1~
Resta: Columna de decenas tomando prestado de las centenas # 1

1. 325 - 41	**2.** 702 - 41	**3.** 713 - 21	**4.** 860 - 70
5. 801 - 91	**6.** 364 - 71	**7.** 302 - 32	**8.** 538 - 85
9. 346 - 54	**10.** 537 - 41		

~<u>Subtraction:Tens Column Borrowing from Hundreds Column #2</u>~

Resta: La columna de las decenas que toma prestada de la columna de las centenas #2

1. 315
  - 21

2. 365
  - 71

3. 804
  - 29

4. 183
  - 91

5. 504
  - 12

6. 406
  - 32

7. 605
  - 62

8. 702
  - 82

9. 624
  - 51

10. 704
  - 42

~Subtraction: Tens Column Borrowing from Hundreds Column #3~

Resta: La columna de las decenas que toma prestada de la columna de las centenas #3

1. 476
   - 81

2. 234
   - 52

3. 643
   - 82

4. 148
   - 92

5. 304
   - 22

6. 417
   - 31

7. 627
   - 42

8. 503
   - 11

9. 642
   - 62

10. 305
    - 73

~Subtraction: Borrowing from the Tens and Hundreds #1~

Resta: Tomando prestado de las decenas y centenas #1

1. 981
  - 267

2. 437
  - 52

3. 260
  - 91

4. 831
  - 92

5. 542
  - 83

6. 791
  - 748

7. 612
  - 89

8. 287
  - 89

9. 612
  - 53

10. 427
  - 89

~Subtraction: Borrowing from the Tens and Hundreds #2~

Resta: Tomando prestado de las decenas y centenas #2

1. 482
  - 93

2. 625
  - 46

3. 324
  - 55

4. 207
  - 28

5. 208
  - 17

6. 334
  - 46

7. 527
  - 69

8. 576
  - 77

9. 204
  - 85

10. 302
  - 14

~*Subtraction: Borrowing from the Tens and Hundreds #3*~

Resta: Tomando prestado de las decenas y centenas #3

1. 814
   - 26

2. 321
   - 32

3. 413
   - 26

4. 884
   - 95

5. 621
   - 37

6. 543
   - 75

7. 843
   - 779

8. 823
   - 88

9. 264
   - 75

10. 823
    - 45

~Subtraction: Borrowing from the Tens and Hundreds #4~

Resta: Tomando prestado de las decenas y centenas #4

1. 704 − 19	**2.** 612 − 43	**3.** 531 − 47	**4.** 825 − 49
5. 641 − 92	**6.** 304 − 98	**7.** 453 − 98	**8.** 724 − 37
9. 415 − 26	**10.** 543 − 97		

Multiplication Overview

There are four lessons in multiplication by multiplying 2 digits by 1 digit. Carrying is involved in multiplication.

A zero is introduced in multiplication. There are two lessons with zeros. A student will find it is easy to multiply with a zero in the middle of two whole numbers.

Examples: 506
          x   4

Step 1: Multiply the multiplicand by the 6 in the multiplier which equals 24.
Step 2: We multiply 500 by 4 and it equals 2000. We Add the two totals together equaling 2,024.

By breaking apart the larger number and multiplying each new number by our multiplier we get our product.

Next, two digits are multiplied by two digits. There are lines below each problem. The first line is for the right number. The second line is for the digit that is on the left side is for the second number.

        42
     x   56
      2 5 2
    + 2 1 0
    | 2 , 3 5 2 |

Step 1. 2 x 6 = 12   *Carry the one and place on top of the 4.
         4 x 6 = 24+1= 25

Step 2. 2 x 5 = 10   *Carry the 1 digit and place on top of the 4.
         4 x 5 = 20 + 1 = 21

Then there are 3 digits times 2 digits. The pattern is the same with three digits. Four lessons with 3 digits times 3 digits. An Example of 3 digits multiplied by 3 digits can be seen below. Prepare a student by showing the process before they solve the problems in multiplication.

Example: 234
              x 567

               _ _ _ _
              _ _ _ _ Z
             _ _ _ _ Z Z
           ____

            1 3 2 , 6 7 8

Step 1:   4 x 7 = 28
                3 x 7 = 21 + 2= 23
                2 x 7 = 14 + 2 =16
                =1,638 *goes on first layer.*
Carried numbers are added to the next column.

Step 2:   4 x 6 = 24
                3 x 6 = 18 + 2= 20
                2 x 6 = 12 + 2= 14
                =1,404 *goes on second layer.*

Step 3:

                4 x 5 = 20
                3 x 5 = 15 + 2 = 17
                2 x 5 = 10 + 1= 11
                =1,170 *goes on final layer.*

Step 4: Add up all layers which will give you the product.

234x567=132,678

Multiplication Worksheets Overview:

- 2 digits times 1 digit
- 3-digit times a single digit
- Zeros: 2-digit times 2 digits
- 3-digit times 3

Descripción general de la multiplicación

Hay cuatro lecciones sobre la multiplicación multiplicando 2 dígitos por 1 dígito. El acarreo está involucrado en la multiplicación.

Se introduce un cero en la multiplicación. Hay dos lecciones con ceros. Un estudiante encontrará que es fácil multiplicar con un cero en medio de dos números enteros.

Exemplos: 506   **Paso 1**: Multiplica el multiplicando por el 6 en el
       x 4   multiplicador que es igual a 24.
      2,024 **Paso 2**: Multiplicamos 500 por 4 y es igual a 2000. Sumamos los dos totales, lo que equivale a 2,024.

Al separar el número más grande y multiplicar cada nuevo número por nuestro multiplicador obtenemos nuestro producto.

A continuación, dos dígitos se multiplican por dos dígitos. Hay líneas debajo de cada problema. La primera línea es para el número correcto. La segunda línea es para el dígito que está en el lado izquierdo es para el segundo número.

    42   **Paso 1.** **2** x 6 = 12 *Lleva el uno y colócalo encima del 4.
   x 56   <u>**4** x 6 = 24+1= 25</u>
   2 5 2
 +2 1 0   **Paso 2.** **2** x 5 = 10 *Lleva el dígito 1 y colócalo encima del 4.
 2, 3 5 2   <u>**4** x 5 = 20 + 1 = 21</u>

Luego hay 3 dígitos multiplicados por 2 dígitos. El patrón es el mismo con tres dígitos. Cuatro lecciones con 3 dígitos multiplicados por 3 dígitos. A continuación se puede ver un ejemplo de 3 dígitos multiplicados por 3 dígitos. Prepare a un estudiante mostrándole el proceso antes de que resuelva los problemas de multiplicación.

Exemplo:
         234
      x 567

```
234
x 567
_ _ _ _
_ _ _ _ Z
_ _ _ _ Z Z
___________
1 3 2 , 6 7 8
```

Paso 1:   4 x 7 = 28
3 x 7 = 21 + 2= 23
2 x 7 = 14 + 2 =16
=1,638 *va en la primera capa.*

** Los números transportados se agregan a la siguiente columna.*

Paso 2:   4 x 6 = 24
3 x 6 = 18 + 2= 20
2 x 6 = 12 + 2= 14
=1,404 *va en la segunda capa.*

Paso 3:

4 x 5 = 20
3 x 5 = 15 + 2 = 17
2 x 5 = 10 + 1= 11
=1,170 *Va a la capa final.*

Paso 4: Suma todas las capas que te darán el producto.
234x567=132,678

Descripción general de la multiplicación:

- 2 dígitos multiplicados por 1 dígito
- 3 dígitos multiplicados por un solo dígito
- Ceros: 2 dígitos por 2 dígitos
- 3 dígitos multiplicados por 3

~Multiplication 1-3 #1~
Multiplicación 1-3 #1

Example:	42	multiplicand	42	multiplicando
	x 2	mutiplier	x 2	multiplicador
	84	product	84	producto

1. 31
x 3

2. 27
x 2

3. 14
x 2

4. 14
x 3

5. 47
x 2

6. 53
x 3

7. 78
x 3

8. 96
x 3

9. 57
x 3

10. 35
x 3

1. 56 x 4	**2.** 43 x 4	**3.** 87 x 4	**4.** 65 x 4
5. 82 x 5	**6.** 64 x 5	**7.** 53 x 5	**8.** 83 x 5
9. 88 x 5	**10.** 66 x 4		

~*Multiplication 6-7 #3*~
Multiplicación 6-7 #3

1. 38
x 6

2. 57
x 7

3. 48
x 6

4. 93
x 7

5. 75
x 6

6. 81
x 7

7. 36
x 6

8. 85
x 7

9. 47
x 6

10. 39
x 7

~*Multiplication 8-9 #4*~
Multiplicación 8-9 #4

1. 23
  x 9

2. 45
  x 8

3. 67
  x 9

4. 89
  x 8

5. 32
  x 8

6. 54
  x 9

7. 76
  x 8

8. 98
  x 9

9. 99
  x 8

10. 10
  x 9

~*Multiplication by Triple Digit #1*~

Multiplicación por Triple Dígito #1

Examples:	507	608	507	608
Ejemplos:	x 4	x 4	x 4	x 4
	28	32	2,028	2,432
	0x	0x		
	+ 20xx	+ 24xx		
	2,028	2,432		

Add up all layers for sum/ Suma todas las capas para sumar.

** X represents the symbol used to illustrate multiplication operation./ X representa el símbolo utilizado para ilustrar la operación de multiplicación*
**You can use a 0, M, or Z when choosing a place holder./ Puede utilizar un 0, una M o una Z al elegir un marcador de posición.*

1. 408
x 2

2. 506
x 3

3. 704
x 8

4. 607
x 4

5. 509
x 2

6. 604
x 6

7. 506
x 9

8. 703
x 5

9. 701
x 7

10. 305
x 1

~*Multiplication by Triple Digit #2*~
Multiplicación por Triple Dígito #2

1. 802 x 7	**2.** 905 x 8	**3.** 503 x 7	**4.** 805 x 6
5. 905 x 9	**6.** 605 x 4	**7.** 403 x 8	**8.** 706 x 5
9. 804 x 3	**10.** 903 x 2		

~*Multiplication 2 by 2 Digits #1*~
~Multiplicación 2 por 2 dígitos #1~

Example: *Ejemplo*:	**1.**	32 x 62 ?	32 x 62 64 + 192x 1984 **Basic**	32 x 62 ⟵ 64 + {18}[12]x 1984 **Broken Down**	**2 x 6 is 12, but you must carry the 10 (1) to the next column. 3x 6 is 18. You'd add the 1 to 18 making it 19.* **2 x 6 es 12, pero debes lleve el 10 (1) al siguiente columna. 3x 6 es 18. Añadirías del 1 al 18, lo que lo convierte en 19.*

1. 34
x 62

2. 54
x 23

3. 97
x 48

4. 56
x 27

5. 32
x 64

6. 82
x 57

7. 18
x 36

8. 54
x 29

9. 54
x 17

10. 28
x 63

~Multiplication 2 by 2 Digits #2~

~Multiplicación 2 por 2 dígitos #2~

1. 54
x 26

2. 63
x 47

3. 16
x 15

4. 49
x 48

5. 86
x 32

6. 55
x 46

7. 73
x 89

8. 43
x 64

9. 94
x 27

10. 64
x 83

~Multiplication 3 by 2 Digits #1~
~Multiplicación 3 por 2 dígitos #1~

Example/:	345	345	345
Ejemplo	x 34	x 34	x 34
	?	[12][16][20]	1380
		+ [9][12][15]x	+ 1035x
		11,730	11,730

Follow the carrying rule as seen on previous pages./Siga la regla de porte como se ve en las páginas anteriores.
Make sure to use a place holder as you multiply over in the next columns./Asegúrate de usar un marcador de posición a medida que multiplicas en las siguientes columnas.

1. 831
x 67

2. 847
x 24

3. 187
x 34

4. 638
x 42

5. 956
x 73

6. 814
x 69

7. 856
x 24

8. 298
x 49

9. 873
x 98

10. 739
x 49

~*Multiplication 3 by 2 Digits #2*~
~*Multiplicación 3 por 2 dígitos #2*~

1. 376
x 41

2. 698
x 23

3. 256
x 44

4. 856
x 37

5. 856
x 48

6. 623
x 98

7. 349
x 86

8. 542
x 35

9. 876
x 56

10. 249
x 76

~Multiplication: 3 Digit Times 3 Digits #1~
~Multiplicación: 3 dígitos por 3 dígitos #1~

**Examples for set up below/Ejemplos de configuración a continuación:*
**This is how you should space each equation and put place holders./ Así es como debes espaciar cada ecuación y poner marcadores de posición.*

1. 321
x 456

_ _ _ _

_ _ _ _ 0

+_ _ _ _ 0 0

2. 748
x 599

_ _ _ _

_ _ _ _ Z = zero

+ _ _ _ _ Z Z = zero

3. 427
x 428

_ _ _ _

_ _ _ Z

+ _ _ _ _ Z Z

4. 507
x 298

_ _ _ _

_ _ _ _ Z

+ _ _ _ _ Z Z

5. 642
x 398

_ _ _ _

_ _ _ _ Z

+ _ _ _ _ Z Z

6. 463
x 287

_ _ _ _

_ _ _ _ Z

+ _ _ _ Z Z

~*Multiplication: 3 Digit Times 3 Digits #2*~
~*Multiplicación: 3 dígitos por 3 dígitos #2*~

**Follow rules and set up as seen on page 93. / Siga las reglas y configúrelo como se ve en la página 93.*
**You can use this set up for 2 by 2 digit multiplication too./También puedes usar esta configuración para la multiplicación de 2 por 2 dígitos.*

1. 432 x 513 _ _ _ _ _ _ _ Z + _ _ _ _ Z Z	**2.** 293 x 598 _ _ _ _ _ _ _ _ Z + _ _ _ _ Z Z	**3.** 486 x 293 _ _ _ _ _ _ _ _ Z + _ _ _ Z Z
4. 327 x 482 _ _ _ _ _ _ _ Z + _ _ _ _ Z Z	**5.** 734 x 279 _ _ _ _ _ _ _ _ Z + _ _ _ _ Z Z	**6.** 278 x 345 _ _ _ _ _ _ _ _ Z + _ _ _ Z Z

~Multiplication: 3 Digit Times 3 Digits #3~
~Multiplicación: 3 dígitos por 3 dígitos #3~

**Follow rules and set up as seen on page 93. / Siga las reglas y configúrelo como se ve en la página 93.*

1. 389
x 784

– – – –
_ _ _ _ Z
+ _ _ _ _ Z Z
____

2. 658
x 249

– – – –
_ _ _ _ Z
+ _ _ _ _ Z Z
____

3. 859
x 678

– – – –
_ _ _ _ Z
+ _ _ _ _ Z Z
____

4. 910
x 863

– – – –
_ _ _ _ Z
+ _ _ _ _ Z Z
____

5. 769
x 478

– – – –
_ _ _ _ Z
+ _ _ _ _ Z Z
____

6. 457
x 398

– – – –
_ _ _ _ Z
+ _ _ _ _ Z Z
____

<u>*Division Overview*</u>

Begin dividing by a single digit number. They need to learn the process and the language that accompanies it. A fact is listed first and it is called the dividend. The next number is called the divisor. The answer to the problems is called the quotient.

In the beginning lessons, the quotient has no remainders. In the next lessons, remainders will happen in the quotient. . Remainders are leftovers when the answer to the problem is not even.

There are three practice pages. The first page involves 2 and 3. Next 4-5, 6-7, and 8-9. However, the next three lessons will have a remainder. Finally, a zero is placed in the dividend. A student will have to work the problem using the knowledge of the previous lessons. A zero will be in the quotient.

Examples:

1.	2.	3.	4.
$2402 \div 2 = \mathbf{1{,}201}$	$12 \div 2 = \mathbf{6}$	$4 \div 2 = \mathbf{2}$	$2 \div 2 = \mathbf{1}$

<u>*DivisionWorksheets Overview*</u>

- Dividing facts evenly.
- 2 digits divided by 1 digit.
- 3 digits divided by single digit.
- Zero in dividend and quotient number.
- Zero creates an even quotient number.

<u>Visión general de la división</u>

Comienza dividiendo por un número de un solo dígito. Necesitan aprender el proceso y el lenguaje que lo acompaña. Un hecho se enumera primero y se llama dividendo. El siguiente número se llama divisor. La respuesta a los problemas se llama cociente.

En las lecciones iniciales, el cociente no tiene restos. En las próximas lecciones, los restos ocurrirán en el cociente. . Los restos son sobras cuando la respuesta al problema no es uniforme.

Hay tres páginas de práctica. La primera página involucra 2 y 3. A continuación, 4-5, 6-7 y 8-9. Sin embargo, las siguientes tres lecciones tendrán un resto. Finalmente, se coloca un cero en el dividendo. Un estudiante tendrá que resolver el problema utilizando el conocimiento de las lecciones anteriores. Un cero estará en el cociente.

Ejemplos:

1.

$2402 \div 2 = \mathbf{1{,}201}$

2.

$12 \div 2 = \mathbf{6}$

3.

$4 \div 2 = \mathbf{2}$

4.

$2 \div 2 = \mathbf{1}$

<u>Visión general de la división</u>

- Dividir los hechos en partes iguales.
- 2 dígitos divididos por 1 dígito.
- 3 dígitos divididos por un solo dígito.
- Cero en número de dividendos y cociente.
- El cero crea un número de cociente par.

~Division: 2-3 #1~
~División: 2-3 #1~

The quotient is even with no remainder in the quotient./ El cociente es par sin residuo en el cociente.

Example/Ejemplo :   * How many groups of 2 can be made from 8? 4 groups
$8 \div 2 = ?$ * ¿Cuántos grupos de 2 se pueden hacer a partir de 8?
(8 = 2+2+2+2) 4 groups

$8 \div 2 = 4$
**Dividend ÷ Divisor = Quotient*   **Dividendo ÷ Divisor = Cociente*

---

1. $10 \div 2 =$ 2. $6 \div 3 =$ 3. $12 \div 2 =$

4. $18 \div 2 =$ 5. $14 \div 2 =$ 6. $9 \div 3 =$

7. $15 \div 3 =$ 8. $14 \div 2 =$ 9. $12 \div 3 =$

10. $16 \div 2 =$

~Division: 4-5 #2~
~División: 4-5 #2~

The quotient is even with no remainder in the quotient./ El cociente es par sin residuo en el cociente.

1. $8 \div 4 =$

2. $15 \div 5 =$

3. $32 \div 4 =$

4. $30 \div 5 =$

5. $20 \div 5 =$

6. $16 \div 4 =$

7. $25 \div 5 =$

8. $20 \div 4 =$

9. $24 \div 4 =$

10. $10 \div 5 =$

~Division: 6-7 #3~

~División: 6-7 #3~

The quotient is even with no remainder in the quotient./ El cociente es par sin residuo en el cociente.

1. $12 \div 6 =$

2. $14 \div 7 =$

3. $18 \div 6 =$

4. $30 \div 6 =$

5. $28 \div 7 =$

6. $6 \div 6 =$

7. $21 \div 7 =$

8. $35 \div 7 =$

9. $24 \div 6 =$

10. $42 \div 7 =$

~Division: 8-9 #4~
~División: 8-9 #4~

The quotient is even with no remainder in the quotient./ El cociente es par sin residuo en el cociente.

1. $16 \div 8 =$ **2.** $27 \div 9 =$ **3.** $45 \div 5 =$

4. $40 \div 8 =$ **5.** $48 \div 8 =$ **6.** $24 \div 8 =$

7. $36 \div 9 =$ **8.** $54 \div 9 =$ **9.** $63 \div 9 =$

10. $32 \div 8 =$

~Division with a Remainder 2-3 #1~
~División con un Remanente 2-3 #1~

A remainder will be in the quotient./Un resto estara en el cociente.

Example/Ejemplo : $7 \div 2 = ?$	* How many groups of 2 can be made from 7? * ¿Cuántos grupos de 2 se pueden hacer a partir de 7? *(7 = 2+2+2+1) 3 with a remaining 1*
$7 \div 2 = 3 R 1$	

1. $7 \div 2 =$ 2. $10 \div 3 =$ 3. $11 \div 2 =$

4. $13 \div 3 =$ 5. $16 \div 3 =$ 6. $9 \div 2 =$

7. $19 \div 2 =$ 8. $22 \div 3 =$ 9. $25 \div 3 =$

10. $28 \div 3 =$

~Division with a Remainder 4-5 #2~
~División con un Remanente 4-5 #2~

A remainder will be in the quotient./Un resto estara en el cociente.

1. $26 \div 5 =$ **2.** $22 \div 4 =$ **3.** $42 \div 5 =$

4. $15 \div 4 =$ **5.** $47 \div 5 =$ **6.** $9 \div 4 =$

7. $5 \div 4 =$ **8.** $27 \div 4 =$ **9.** $16 \div 5 =$

10. $13 \div 4 =$

~Division with a Remainder 6-7 #3~
~División con un Remanente 6-7 #3~

***A remainder will be in the quotient./Un resto estara en el cociente.**

1. $15 \div 6 =$

2. $16 \div 7 =$

3. $38 \div 6 =$

4. $29 \div 7 =$

5. $43 \div 6 =$

6. $27 \div 6 =$

7. $58 \div 7 =$

8. $22 \div 7 =$

9. $32 \div 6 =$

10. $50 \div 7 =$

~Division with a Remainder 8-9 #4~
~División con un Remanente 8-9 #4~

**A remainder will be in the quotient./Un resto estara en el cociente.*

1. $74 \div 8 =$ **2.** $20 \div 9 =$ **3.** $42 \div 8 =$

4. $38 \div 9 =$ **5.** $84 \div 9 =$ **6.** $66 \div 8 =$

7. $28 \div 9 =$ **8.** $35 \div 8 =$ **9.** $47 \div 9 =$

10. $57 \div 8 =$

~Division Even Quotient 2-3 #1~
~Cociente par de división 2-3 #1~

Example/Ejemplo:

1.	2.	3.	4.
$2 \div 1 = 2$	$12 \div 2 = 6$	$4 \div 2 = 2$	$6 \div 3 = 2$

Dividend ÷ Divisor = Quotient   *Dividendo ÷ Divisor = Cociente*

Division quotient will be even./El cociente de division sera par.

1. $104 \div 2 =$

2. $39 \div 3 =$

3. $153 \div 3 =$

4. $219 \div 3 =$

5. $213 \div 3 =$

6. $148 \div 2 =$

7. $249 \div 3 =$

8. $144 \div 2 =$

9. $168 \div 2 =$

10. $27 \div 3 =$

~Division Even Quotient 4-5 #2~
~Cociente par de división 4-5 #2~

***Division quotient will be even./El cociente de division sera par.**

1. $48 \div 4 =$

2. $255 \div 5 =$

3. $324 \div 4 =$

4. $105 \div 5 =$

5. $164 \div 4 =$

6. $155 \div 5 =$

7. $368 \div 4 =$

8. $208 \div 4 =$

9. $155 \div 5 =$

10. $204 \div 4 =$

~Division Even Quotient 6-7 #3~
~Cociente par de división 6-7 #3~

***Division quotient will be even./El cociente de division sera par.**

1. $366 \div 6 =$ 2. $497 \div 7 =$ 3. $306 \div 6 =$

4. $497 \div 7 =$ 5. $126 \div 6 =$ 6. $147 \div 7 =$

7. $192 \div 6 =$ 8. $504 \div 7 =$ 9. $372 \div 6 =$

10. $364 \div 7 =$

~Division Even Quotient 8-9 #4~
~Cociente par de división 8-9 #4~

***Division quotient will be even./El cociente de division sera par.**

1. $416 \div 8 =$ **2.** $549 \div 9 =$ **3.** $256 \div 8 =$

4. $468 \div 9 =$ **5.** $279 \div 9 =$ **6.** $248 \div 8 =$

7. $288 \div 9 =$ **8.** $819 \div 9 =$ **9.** $168 \div 8 =$

10. $656 \div 8 =$

~Division: 2-3 with Zero in the Answer #1~

~División: 2-3 con cero en la respuesta #1~

1. $2103 \div 3 =$

2. $1004 \div 2 =$

3. $909 \div 3 =$

4. $408 \div 2 =$

5. $2409 \div 3 =$

6. $1204 \div 2 =$

7. $2406 \div 3 =$

8. $1404 \div 2 =$

9. $2709 \div 3 =$

10. $1606 \div 2 =$

~*Division: 4-5 with Zero in the Answer #2*~
~División: 4-5 con cero en la respuesta #2~

1. $1208 \div 4 =$ **2.** $1005 \div 5 =$ **3.** $404 \div 4 =$

4. $1505 \div 5 =$ **5.** $2004 \div 4 =$ **6.** $2005 \div 5 =$

7. $1604 \div 4 =$ **8.** $2505 \div 5 =$ **9.** $2408 \div 4 =$

10. $3005 \div 5 =$

~*Division: 6-7 with Zero in the Answer #3*~

~*División: 6-7 con cero en la respuesta #3*~

1. $606 \div 6 =$ **2.** $707 \div 7 =$ **3.** $1206 \div 6 =$

4. $2107 \div 7 =$ **5.** $1206 \div 6 =$ **6.** $2107 \div 7 =$

7. $3606 \div 6 =$ **8.** $3507 \div 7 =$ **9.** $2406 \div 6 =$

10. $3507 \div 7 =$

1. 2408 ÷ 8 =

2. 8109 ÷ 9 =

3. 3208 ÷ 8 =

4. 4509 ÷ 9 =

5. 4008 ÷ 8 =

6. 4505 ÷ 5 =

7. 6408 ÷ 8 =

8. 2709 ÷ 9 =

9. 4808 ÷ 8 =

10. 5409 ÷ 9 =

~Division 2-3 with a Remainder #1~
~División 2-3 con un Resto #1~

1. $115 \div 2 =$

2. $106 \div 3 =$

3. $135 \div 4 =$

4. $157 \div 2 =$

5. $136 \div 3 =$

6. $177 \div 2 =$

7. $175 \div 3 =$

8. $137 \div 2 =$

9. $223 \div 3 =$

10. $197 \div 2 =$

~*Division 4-5 with a Remainder #2*~
~*División 4-5 con un Resto #2*~

1. $93 \div 4 =$

2. $116 \div 5 =$

3. $255 \div 4 =$

4. $211 \div 5 =$

5. $135 \div 4 =$

6. $312 \div 5 =$

7. $467 \div 5 =$

8. $177 \div 4 =$

9. $411 \div 5 =$

10. $210 \div 4 =$

~*Division 6-7 with a Remainder #3*~
~*División 6-7 con un Resto #3*~

1. $134 \div 6 =$ **2.** $158 \div 7 =$ **3.** $435 \div 6 =$

4. $226 \div 7 =$ **5.** $167 \div 6 =$ **6.** $377 \div 7 =$

7. $225 \div 6 =$ **8.** $417 \div 7 =$ **9.** $377 \div 6 =$

10. $508 \div 7 =$

~*Division 8-9 with a Remainder #4*~
~*División 8-9 con un Resto #4*~

1. $97 \div 8 =$ **2.** $109 \div 9 =$ **3.** $259 \div 8 =$

4. $197 \div 9 =$ **5.** $103 \div 8 =$ **6.** $286 \div 9 =$

7. $339 \div 8 =$ **8.** $379 \div 9 =$ **9.** $490 \div 8 =$

10. $476 \div 9 =$

Final Summary

After many years of teaching and observing students and their weakness in the math area, I developed with what I believe to be an easy path for students to learn the addition, subtraction, multiplication, and division facts in elementary school.

Students will learn at their own pace and will take a timed paper test, once they can pass the oral test. No child will be left behind when an adult holds a child accountable in class. By coaching a child each day, the child will become a happy student. Now, we also have paraprofessionals which can help guide and keep students on track. Remember to use index cards to memorize and practice all math facts. Which can be used later to review and practice.

Although computers are used in the classroom, the math lessons in American Rocket Math may be utilized with students who may struggle with the different concepts being introduced in the classroom. American Rocket Math covers the areas that students struggle with in the classroom.

It is my hope that by using my program students will be at grade level if not be advanced in all struggling math areas. I provided support and work in all the various areas students are known to struggle with. I believe in my program, and I believe in your students' ability to learn. Together we can help get your students to the level of success we know they can reach!

Resumen final

Después de muchos años de enseñar y observar a los estudiantes y sus debilidades en el área de matemáticas, desarrollé lo que creo que es un camino fácil para que los estudiantes aprendan las operaciones de suma, resta, multiplicación y división en la escuela primaria.

Los estudiantes aprenderán a su propio ritmo y realizarán una prueba en papel cronometrada, una vez que puedan aprobar la prueba oral. Ningún niño se quedará atrás cuando un adulto responsabilice a un niño en clase. Al entrenar a un niño todos los días, el niño se convertirá en un estudiante feliz. Ahora también contamos con paraprofesionales que pueden ayudar a guiar y mantener a los estudiantes en el buen camino.

Aunque las computadoras se utilizan en el aula, las lecciones de matemáticas en American Rocket Math se pueden utilizar con estudiantes que pueden tener dificultades con los diferentes conceptos que se introducen en el aula. American Rocket Math cubre las áreas con las que los estudiantes luchan en el aula. Recuerde usar fichas para memorizar y practicar todas las operaciones matemáticas. Lo cual se puede utilizar más adelante para repasar y practicar.

Tengo la esperanza de que al usar mi programa, los estudiantes estén al nivel de su grado, si no avanzan, en todas las áreas de matemáticas. Brindé apoyo y trabajo en todas las áreas en las que se sabe que los estudiantes tienen dificultades. Creo en mi programa y creo en la capacidad de aprendizaje de sus estudiantes. ¡Juntos podemos ayudar a que sus estudiantes alcancen el nivel de éxito que sabemos que pueden alcanzar!

<u>Answer Key Pages:</u>

Page 18- Row 1: 1, 4, 7, 10, 8, 6.
            Row 2: 5, 6, 3, 9, 9, 4.
            Row 3: 7, 10, 7 11, 11, 9.
            Row 4: 6, 5, 8, 12, 2, 11.
            Row 5: 2, 8, 10, 10, 3, 12.

Page 19- Row 1: 12, 10, 11, 13, 8.
            Row 2: 11, 7 , 12, 9, 8.
            Row 3: 6, 10, 6, 7, 13.
            Row 4: 9, 5, 5, 14, 4.

Page 20- Row 1: 13, 11, 9, 16, 11
            Row 2: 14, 10, 8, 12, 9.
            Row 3: 6, 15, 15, 12, 7.
            Row 4: 8, 7, 10, 14, 13.

Page 21- Row 1: 8, 18, 13, 13, 15.
            Row 2: 16, 11, 16, 12, 12.
            Row 3: 10, 15, 9, 9, 17.
            Row 4: 14, 14, 17, 11, 10.

Page 24- Row 1: 0, 2, 0, 3, 2.
            Row 2: 1, 1, 1, 0, 0.

Page 25- Row 1: 3, 2, 1, 4.
            Row 2: 3, 4, 1, 0.
            Row 3: 5, 2, 0.

Page 26- Row 1: 4, 4, 1, 7, 5.
            Row 2: 2, 6, 1, 6, 0.
            Row 3: 2, 5, 3, 0, 3.

Page 27- Row 1: 6, 6, 4, 4, 2.
            Row 2: 7, 3, 1, 0, 7.
            Row 3: 2, 3, 1, 8, 5.
            Row 4: 7, 0, 5, 8.

Page 32- Row 1: 2, 9, 10, 7, 0, 24.
Row 2: 6, 24, 4, 12, 8, 18.
Row 3: 9, 12, 18, 21, 0, 3.
Row 4: 14, 18, 16, 15, 0, 6.
Row 5: 15, 0, 12, 3, 27, 12.

Page 33- Row 1: 5, 12, 0, 25, 35, 20.
Row 2: 40, 15, 28, 30, 24, 32.
Row 3: 30, 16, 32, 4, 0, 40.
Row 4: 24, 8, 10, 20, 45, 36.

Page 34- Row 1: 6, 21, 24, 0, 30.
Row 2: 35, 36, 28, 49, 56.
Row 3: 63, 7, 54, 48, 42.
Row 4: 12, 49, 0, 14, 18.

Page 35- Row 1: 0, 18, 64, 54, 27.
Row 2: 63, 48, 32, 56, 45.
Row 3: 0, 8, 40, 81, 72.
Row 4: 16, 9, 24, 36, 81.

Page 37- Row 1: 0, 44, 50, 66, 48, 72, 36.
Row 2: 132, 11, 55, 100, 20, 70, 22.
Row 3: 48, 84, 12, 0, 90, 33, 77.
Row 4: 110, 24, 60, 132, 110, 40, 99.
Row 5: 88, 120, 30, 120, 121, 108, 144.
Row 6: 60, 80, 0, 10, 96.

Page 38- Row 1: 9, 28, 40, 72, 121, 48, 60.
Row 2: 42, 48, 110, 49, 132, 36, 42.
Row 3: 120, 21, 63, 63, 64, 24, 54.
Row 4: 56, 18, 32, 24, 36, 70, 96.
Row 5: 81, 36, 45, 16, 35, 144, 120.
Row 6: 25, 27, 12, 30, 20, 72, 99.

Page 39- On the Farm

       1. 71 chickens.

       2. 22 pigs.

       3. $10.00

       4. 29 cats.

       5. 10 dogs.

Page 40- Trees

       1. 76 walnut trees.

       2. 84 almond trees.

       3. 47 pistachio trees.

       4. 7 more men.

       5. 18 more workers.

Page 41- Super Store

       1. 20 packages.

       2. 50 basketballs.

       3. 9 car kits.

       4. 16 toy soldiers.

       5. 26 candy bars.

Page 42- Farmers Market

       1. 36 baskets.

       2. 81 watermelons.

       3. 13 cantaloupes.

       4. 20 onions.

       5. 97 tomatoes.

Page 43- Grocery store

       1. $18.13.

       2. $76.05

       3. $139.93

       4. $39.60

       5. $10.17

Page 44- The Big Garden
       1. 18 pumpkin seeds.
       2. 20 cantaloupes.
       3. $7,500.
       4. $11,040.
       5. 15 onions.

Page 45- Chips and More Chips
       1. 5 in each.
       2. 8 more hours.
       3. 5 bags each.
       4. 8 bags each.
       5. 6 rows.

Page 50- Row 1: 11, 12, 13, 13, 25.
       Row 2: 12, 14, 14, 12, 15.
       Row 3: 16, 13, 26, 31, 24.
       Row 4: 34, 36, 35, 22, 33.

Page 51- Row 1: 27, 16, 34, 59, 47.
       Row 2: 58, 45, 49, 46, 18.
       Row 3: 29, 56, 35, 26, 27.
       Row 4: 26, 36, 29, 49, 59.

Page 52- Row 1: 51, 42, 31, 53, 80.
       Row 2: 33, 63, 81, 62, 80.
       Row 3: 71, 64, 70, 82, 60.
       Row 4: 82, 65, 86, 52, 82.

Page 53- Row 1: 108, 62, 84, 94, 67.
       Row 2: 97, 76, 76, 82, 101.
       Row 3: 105, 83, 101, 80, 52.
       Row 4: 93, 100, 40, 95, 65.

Page 54- Row 1: 152, 102, 111, 80.
       Row 2: 115, 71, 181, 142.
       Row 3: 71, 142, 111, 121.

Page 55- Row 1: 142, 71, 90, 110.
   Row 2: 86, 111, 142, 110.
   Row 3: 71, 110, 83, 87.

Page 56- Row 1: 74, 100, 114, 102.
   Row 2: 83, 125, 121, 111.
   Row 3: 102, 95, 142, 165.

Page 57- Row 1: 146, 164, 175, 175.
   Row 2: 163, 152, 148, 92.
   Row 3: 142, 133, 193, 195.

Page 58- Row 1: 137, 149, 139, 171.
   Row 2: 124, 131, 113, 194.
   Row 3: 110, 182, 183, 211.

Page 59- Row 1: 131, 185, 183, 120.
   Row 2: 172, 148, 150, 128.
   Row 3: 155, 205, 180, 198.

Page 60- Row 1: 601, 1,223, 720, 720.
   Row 2: 613, 922, 441, 543.
   Row 3: 1,302, 833

Page 61- Row 1: 800, 1,020, 827, 921.
   Row 2: 674, 733, 810, 680.
   Row 3: 745, 1,040.

Page 62- Row 1: 521, 1,091, 1,038, 945.
   Row 2: 1,045, 1,225, 441, 1,134.
   Row 3: 646, 922.

Page 63- Row 1: 1,117, 1,529, 1,414, 1,227.
   Row 2: 2,385, 1,506, 1,376, 1,257.
   Row 3: 1,538, 1,915.

Page 64- Row 1: 951, 2,003, 1,338, 1,443.
   Row 2: 1,276, 1,640, 1,452, 958.
   Row 3: 1,144, 2,326.

Page 65- Row 1: 1,740, 1,173, 1,633, 1,289.
         Row 2: 1,884, 1,493, 1,421, 1,598.
         Row 3: 1,619, 1,503.

Page 66- 1: 6, A-4, B-2.
         2: 13, A-8, B-5.
         3: 11, A-2, B-9.
         4: 13, A-8, B-5.

Page 67- 1: 12, A-4, B-8.
         2: 13, A-6, B-7.
         3: 13, A-4, B-9.
         4: 13, A-5, B-8.
         5: 17, A-8, B-9.

Page 68- 1: 8, A-1, B-7.
         2: 9, A-4, B-5.
         3: 14, A-6, B-8.
         4: 15, A-7, B-8.
         5: 17, A-9, B-8.

Page 69- 1: A. 47-38=9, B. 9.
         2: A. 101-85=16, B.16.
         3: A. 93-76=17, B. 17.
         4: A. 101-45=56, B. 56.
         5: A. 145-79=66, B. 66.

Page 70- 1: A. 73-36=37, B. 37.
         2: A. 78-43=35, B.35.
         3: A. 97-28=69, B. 69.
         4: A. 99-83=16, B. 16.
         5: A. 47-23=24, B. 24.

Page 71- 1: A. 89-73=16, B. 16.
         2: A. 101-64=37, B.37.
         3: A. 38-17=21, B. 21.
         4: A. 46-23=23, B. 23.
         5: A. 99-84=15, B. 15.

Page 72- 1: A. 4+5+4=13, B. 26-13=13, C. 13.
2: A. 5+9+8=22, B. 31-22=9, C. 9.
3: A. 4+6+9=19, B. 43-19=24, C. 24.
4: A. 8+9+8=25, B. 58-25=33, C. 33.
5: A. 4+6+9=19, B. 78-19=59, C. 59.

Page 73- 1: A. 8+3+9+7=27, B. 76-27=49, C. 49.
2: A. 4+5+6+9=24, B. 80-24=56, C. 56.
3: A. 9+7+3=19, B. 24-19=5, C. 5.
4: A. 6+4+9=19, B. 33-19=14, C. 14.
5: A. 7+9+6+8=30, B. 44-30=14, C. 14.

Page 74- 1: A. 8+3+9=20, B. 76-20=56, C. 56.
2: A. 4+5+6+9=24, B. 82-24=58, C. 58.
3: A. 9+7+3=19, B. 82-19=5=63, C. 63.
4: A. 6+4+9=19, B. 30-19=11, C. 11.
5: A. 7+9+6+8=30, B. 45-30=15, C. 15.

Page 78- Row 1: 39, 49, 27, 69.
Row 2: 38, 79, 45, 69.
Row 3: 69, 38.

Page 79- Row 1: 29, 19, 77, 87.
Row 2: 78, 59, 48, 28.
Row 3: 54, 76.

Page 80- Row 1: 89, 15, 48, 69.
Row 2: 67, 49, 69, 18.
Row 3: 29, 66.

Page 81- Row 1: 46, 787, 689, 349.
Row 2: 679, 276, 777, 319.
Row 3: 499, 639.

Page 82- Row 1: 400, 799, 599, 499.
Row 2: 299, 398, 599, 299.
Row 3: 599, 698.

Page 83- Row 1: 299, 399, 799, 798.
        Row 2: 697, 395, 399, 597.
        Row 3: 498, 597.

Page 84- Row 1: 297, 799, 699, 899.
        Row 2: 395, 599, 698, 399.
        Row 3: 798, 199.

Page 85- Row 1: 7,999, 1,998, 3,999, 5,997.
        Row 2: 6,996, 7,994, 1,992, 2,993.
        Row 3: 995, 4,991.

Page 86- Row 1: 59,998, 79,999, 49,995, 89,997.
        Row 2: 29,996, 9,994, 69,993, 39,991.
        Row 3: 19,998, 59,997.

Page 87- Row 1: 99,999, 699,998, 299,996, 399,995.
        Row 2: 799,991, 199,997, 899,996, 599,993.
        Row 3: 699,999, 499,995.

Page 88- Row 1: 284, 661, 692, 790.
        Row 2: 710, 293, 270, 453.
        Row 3: 292, 496.

Page 89- Row 1: 294, 294, 775, 92.
        Row 2: 492, 374, 543, 620.
        Row 3: 573, 662.

Page 90- Row 1: 395, 182, 561, 56.
        Row 2: 282, 386, 585, 492.
        Row 3: 580, 232.

Page 91- Row 1: 714, 385, 169, 739.
        Row 2: 459, 43, 523, 198.
        Row 3: 559, 338.

Page 92- Row 1: 389, 579, 269, 179.
        Row 2: 191, 288, 458, 499.
        Row 3: 119, 288.

Page 93- Row 1: 788, 289, 387, 789.
       Row 2: 584, 468, 64, 735.
       Row 3: 189, 778.

Page 94- Row 1: 685, 569, 484, 776.
       Row 2: 549, 206, 355, 687.
       Row 3: 389, 446.

Page 99- Row 1: 93, 54, 28, 42.
       Row 2: 94, 159, 234, 288.
       Row 3: 171, 105.

Page 100- Row 1: 224, 172, 348, 260.
       Row 2: 410, 320, 265, 415.
       Row 3: 440, 264.

Page 101- Row 1: 228, 399, 288, 651.
       Row 2: 450, 567, 216, 595.
       Row 3: 282, 273.

Page 102- Row 1: 207, 360, 603, 712.
       Row 2: 256, 486, 608, 882.
       Row 3: 792, 90.

Page 103- Row 1: 816, 1,518, 5,632, 2,428.
       Row 2: 1,018, 3,624, 4,554, 3,515.
       Row 3: 4,907, 305.

Page 104- Row 1: 5,614, 7,240, 3,521, 4,830.
       Row 2: 8,145, 2,420, 3,224, 3,530.
       Row 3: 2,412, 1,806.

Page 105- Row 1: 2,108, 1,242, 4,656, 1,512.
       Row 2: 2,048, 4,674, 648, 1,566.
       Row 3: 918, 1,764.

Page 106- Row 1: 1,404, 2,961, 240, 2,352.
       Row 2: 2,752, 2,530, 6,497, 2,752.
       Row 3: 2,538, 5,312.

Page 107- Row 1: 55,677, 20,328, 6,358, 26,796.
          Row 2: 69,788, 56,166, 20,544, 14,602.
          Row 3: 85,554, 36,211.

Page 108- Row 1: 15,416, 16,054, 11,264, 31,672.
          Row 2: 41,088, 61,504, 30,014, 18,970.
          Row 3: 49,056, 18,924.

Page 109- Row 1: 146,376, 448,052, 182,756.
          Row 2: 151,086, 255,516, 132,881.

Page 110- Row 1: 221,616, 175,214, 142,398.
          Row 2: 157,614, 204,786, 95,910.

Page 111- Row 1: 304,976, 163,842, 582,402.
          Row 2: 785,330, 367,582, 181,886.

Page 114- Row 1: 5, 2, 6.
          Row 2: 9, 7 , 3.
          Row 3: 5, 7, 4.
          Row 4: 8.

Page 115- Row 1: 2, 3, 8.
          Row 2: 6, 4, 4.
          Row 3: 5, 5, 6.
          Row 4: 2.

Page 116- Row 1: 2, 2, 3.
          Row 2: 5, 4, 1.
          Row 3: 3, 5, 4.
          Row 4: 6.

Page 117- Row 1: 2, 3, 9.
          Row 2: 5, 6, 3.
          Row 3: 4, 6, 7.
          Row 4: 4.

Page 118- Row 1: 3 r1, 3 r1, 5 r1.
Row 2: 4 r1, 5 r1, 4 r1.
Row 3: 9 r1, 7 r1, 8 r1.
Row 4: 9 r1.

Page 119- Row 1: 5 r1, 5 r2, 8 r2.
Row 2: 3 r3, 9 r2, 2 r1.
Row 3: 1 r1, 6 r3, 3 r1.
Row 4: 3 r1.

Page 120- Row 1: 2 r3, 2 r2, 6 r2.
Row 2: 4 r1, 7 r1, 4 r3.
Row 3: 8 r2, 3 r1, 5 r2.
Row 4: 7 r1.

Page 121- Row 1: 9 r2, 2 r2, 5 r2.
Row 2: 4 r2, 9 r3, 8 r2.
Row 3: 3 r1, 4 r3, 5 r2.
Row 4: 7 r1.

Page 122- Row 1: 52, 13, 51.
Row 2: 73, 71, 74.
Row 3: 83, 72, 84.
Row 4: 9.

Page 123- Row 1: 12, 51, 81.
Row 2: 21, 41, 31.
Row 3: 92, 52, 31.
Row 4: 51.

Page 124- Row 1: 61, 71, 51.
Row 2: 71, 21, 21.
Row 3: 32, 72, 62.
Row 4: 52.

Page 125- Row 1: 52, 61, 32.
Row 2: 52, 31, 31.
Row 3: 32, 91, 21.
Row 4: 82.

Page 126- Row 1: 701, 502, 303.
          Row 2: 204, 803, 602.
          Row 3: 802, 702, 903.
          Row 4: 803.

Page 127- Row 1: 302, 201, 101.
          Row 2: 301, 501, 401.
          Row 3: 401, 501, 602.
          Row 4: 601.

Page 128- Row 1: 101, 101, 201.
          Row 2: 301, 201, 301.
          Row 3: 601, 501, 401.
          Row 4: 501.

Page 129- Row 1: 301, 901, 401.
          Row 2: 501, 501, 901.
          Row 3: 801, 301, 601.
          Row 4: 601.

Page 130- Row 1: 57 r1, 35 r1, 33 r3.
          Row 2: 78 r1, 45 r1, 88 r1.
          Row 3: 58 r1, 68 r1, 74 r1.
          Row 4: 98 r1.

Page 131- Row 1: 23 r1, 23 r1, 63 r3.
          Row 2: 42 r1, 33 r3, 62 r2.
          Row 3: 93 r2, 44 r1, 82 r1.
          Row 4: 52 r2.

Page 132- Row 1: 22 r2, 22 r4, 72 r3.
          Row 2: 32 r2, 27 r5, 53 r6.
          Row 3: 37 r3, 59 r4, 62 r5.
          Row 4: 72 r4.

Page 133- Row 1: 12 r1, 12 r1, 32 r3.
          Row 2: 21 r8, 12 r7, 31 r7.
          Row 3: 42 r3, 42 r1, 61 r2.
          Row 4: 52 r8.

Bibliography

- Eugene D. Nichols, Paul A. Anderson, Leslie a Dwight, Frances Flournoy, Robert Kalin, John Schluep, Leonard Simon, <u>Holt School Mathematics Teacher's Edition, Holt, Rinehart and Winston, Inc.</u> New York, 1974.

- Stephen S. Willoughby, E.D., Carl Bereiter, Ph.D., Peter Hilton, Ph.D. Joseph H. Rubinstein, Ph.D. <u>Real Math</u>, Open Court, La Salle, Illinois, 1981.

- Audrey V. Buffington, Alice R. Garr, Jay Graening, Phillip P Halloran, Michael L. Mahaffey, Mary O'Neal, <u>Merrill Mathematics</u>, Charles E. Merrill Publishing Company, Columbus, Ohio, 1985

- L. Carey Bolster, Gloria Felix Cox, E. Glenadine Gibb, Viggo P. Hansen, Joan E. Kirkpatrick, Charles R. McNerney, David F. Robitaille, Harold C. Trimble, Irvin E. Vance, Ray Walch, Robert J. Wisner, <u>Mathematics Around Us</u>, Scott, Foresman and Company, Illinois, 1975.

- Stephen Hake, John Saxon, <u>Saxon Math 54</u>, Saxon Publishers, Inc., Norman Oklahoma, 2001.

- Stephen Jake, John Saxon, <u>Saxon Math 65</u>, Saxon Publishers, Inc., Norman Oklahoma, 1995.

- Corporate Group, <u>English to Spanish Translation of Sentences, Google</u>, November 26, 2023.

- Corporate Group, <u>English to Spanish Translation of Sentences, Google</u>, December 2, 2023.